Contemporary
Labor Relations

Philip L. Martin
University of California, Davis

Wadsworth Publishing Company, Inc.
Belmont, California

Printed in the United States of America

1 2 3 4 5 6 7 8 9 10—83 82 81 80 79

Library of Congress Cataloging in Publication Data

Martin, Philip L., 1949–
   Contemporary labor relations.

   Includes bibliographies and index.
   1. Industrial relations—United States.
2. Trade-unions—United States. I. Title.
HD8072.M297   331'.0973   78-26138
ISBN 0-534-00688-4

Preface

This is a book about conflict, the inevitable conflict between worker and employer that arises with the exchange of effort for reward. The interests of employers, concerned with production and profit, collide with the goals of employees, who seek income, security, and status. Government assumes multiple roles. It defines the legal framework within which labor and management interact, erects protective labor legislation to provide minimum health, wage, and safety standards, and bargains directly with its growing work force. The result is a system, composed of employers, labor organizations, and government, for resolving the natural labor conflicts in society.

The American labor relations system has been quite successful in permitting increases in productivity, output, and earnings. Most labor conflicts are resolved quickly and peacefully, accounting for their low public visibility. But some conflicts erupt into strikes, pickets, and/or lockouts. Rather than examining instances of agreement or disagreement, we erect a framework for analyzing the sources of inevitable labor conflict, the history and structure of the contending parties, and the use of collective bargaining to achieve temporary accord.

Several themes dominate this book. The central theme is that labor conflict is an inevitable part of employment and production. This labor conflict must be resolved if wages are to be earned or profits obtained. While the nature of employment and production gives rise to labor conflict, the interdependency between worker and employer simultaneously promotes cooperation to assure the labor peace that workers and employers require to enjoy the rewards of production—wages and profits. At each stage in the evolution of labor relations, the structure of the economy combines with sociopolitical attitudes to affect the nature, processes, and outcomes of the labor relations system. Every society has *some* system for resolving labor conflict. International comparisons are provided to highlight the uniqueness of the American labor relations system, including its reliance on localized bargaining between unions and employers, its conviction that there should be only one union per industry or occupation (exclusive jurisdiction), and its traditional preference for economic instruments to achieve concessions.

This book is intended to provide the economics, business, or law student with an introduction to the salient aspects of contemporary labor relations. Although no previous knowledge of labor economics or labor relations is necessary, the book assumes sufficient student motivation to require careful reading of a short text rather than the digestion of a voluminous tome. The aim has been to provide a clear and concise introduction, but an introduction with sufficient depth to permit the interested student to move directly into more specialized courses in collective bargaining, trade unionism, labor economics, or business and law courses.

As with all such literary enterprises, this book would have suffered without the insights of colleagues and reviewers. My greatest intellectual debt is to Jack Barbash. His teaching first stimulated my interest in labor problems, and he has improved this book with a variety of useful suggestions. For helpful comments on early versions of several chapters, I am indebted to Bruce Hall and Charles Craver. Mark Martin read the entire manuscript and deserves thanks for detecting awkward phrases. The following reviewers provided helpful feedback: Gerald Glyde, Pennsylvania State University; James Koch, University of Oregon; Thomas Kochan, Cornell University; Howard Leftwich, University of Cincinnati; Ian McAndrew, California State University, Sacramento; Karl Magnusen, Florida International University; Allan Rosenberg, West Liberty State College; David Shapiro, Ohio State University; William D. Torrence, University of Nebraska; Lane Tracy, Ohio University; Peter A. Veglahn, Clarkson College of Technology; and Kenneth Wheeler, University of Minnesota. Three anonymous reviewers provided a variety of useful comments.

Philip L. Martin

Contents

For my parents

INTRODUCTION

1

Modern societies contain numerous individuals and groups with a wide diversity of goals. Many of these goals are mutually incompatible (e.g., at a point in time, more wages may mean fewer profits), producing inevitable conflicts of interest as competing groups attempt to achieve their particular aims. Social stability requires that such conflicts be resolved peacefully, and society has evolved a variety of institutional devices for accomplishing this end. Disputes between individuals can be settled through the legal process, political disagreements can be resolved with legislative compromises, and employment conflicts can be minimized through **negotiation** between labor institutions. Conflict is an inevitable part of a society comprised of individuals and groups with divergent purposes; it is in the means used to resolve these conflicts that societies differ.

Labor Relations Systems

Labor relations encompass those conflicts which arise as a result of employment and production. Three conflicting interests are involved: entrepreneurial interests in production and profit, worker interests in economic welfare and dignity, and the public interest in ensuring prosperity and stability. These broad interests inevitably collide. The study of labor relations is an examination of the structure and functioning of the devices which arise to resolve these inevitable conflicts. Since each society attempts to resolve labor conflict in its own way, a variety of labor institutions exists.

The very factors which give rise to labor conflict also promote cooperation between employers and unions. Employers strive for efficiency and profits, but production and profits arise only if the labor force agrees to work. Just as employers are dependent on workers to achieve profits, workers require employers to provide employment and wages. The clash of worker and employer goals gives rise to potential labor conflict, but the interdependency between worker and employer also promotes long-term cooperation, since both sides lose during conflict phases of the labor-management relationship. When exploring the sources of labor conflict, it is important to remember that the

1

parties have a very strong dependency relationship, one which counters incentives for continual conflict and assures periods of labor peace.

Labor is the only productive input which requires such an elaborate system to govern the exchange of effort for reward. Among all productive inputs, labor is unique because (1) the worker cannot be separated from his work, forcing a *continual* bargain over actual levels of individual effort on-the-job; (2) the worker is both producer and consumer; and (3) the individual is the basic constituent element of a democratic society. The fact that each individual plays multiple roles in society makes the labor transaction, in which the isolated individual is relatively powerless, one of the most complex in the economy.

In the past, the system which links workers and employers in the labor transaction was often termed "industrial relations," reflecting the emergence of modern labor problems with large-scale industry. The realization that labor problems are just as critical in the now-dominant service sector has led to the more generic term of "labor relations." A labor relations system can be described by its *inputs,* the number, structure, and distribution of unions and managements, its *processes,* including the coverage and content of collective agreements as well as the political activities of labor and management, and its *outcomes,* the levels of earnings, productivity, and output which are achieved. The immediate outcomes of labor relations systems, the incidence and duration of **strikes,** and the handling of workplace grievances are incomplete comparative measures of the effectiveness of labor relations systems, although these outcomes are vital for day-to-day labor-management interaction.

The three-part framework of inputs, processes, and outcomes simplifies a complex system. At any point in time, the interaction of inputs and outcomes is linked by ongoing labor processes, which in turn affect the number and functioning of unions and managements. These feedback mechanisms make simple causal analysis of a labor relations system at a single point in time very difficult. But the system and its interacting components are merely one slice of a transaction which has evolved over decades. In few other exchanges are traditions so important for current behavior; hence, a description of the current system is usually prefaced by a historical overview.

The element of the system which receives most attention is the *trade union,* the workers' own organization. A few salient aspects of trade unions are worth remembering. Unions began as *defensive reactions* to changes initiated by others. Since unions cannot create jobs, they serve as limited-purpose institutions (except for revolutionary unions), designed to exert control over existing jobs rather than assuming management roles themselves. Even this limited union role was granted with reluctance. Unions began as illegal associations, enjoying the status of legal entities under a defined regulative framework only since 1935. Few organizations so important in society are still so controversial. In America, labor unions represent only a minority of the labor force, but even this limited power base has made organized labor the most important voice on labor issues and on many other policy issues as well.

In American labor relations, unions and managements have worked out their differences with varying degrees of government intervention. As the mass of the American labor force moved from agriculture to industry, public policy changed from hostility toward unions to embracing **collective bargaining,** erecting a legal framework within which competing interests could be resolved. The rise of the service economy and increased public employment as well as concern for macroeconomic stability and civil rights led to a new injection of public involvement in labor relations in the 1960s and 1970s. Today, the public interest in labor relations goes far beyond a mere framework or rule-setting role. Government now intervenes in the employment process to assure equal employment opportunities and to ensure that the outcomes of the bargaining process are compatible with national economic policies. In addition, governments at federal, state, and local levels bargain with the burgeoning public sector work force, now totaling some 15 million persons.

The growing role of government in resolving labor conflicts reflects its own importance as an employer and an increased willingness to intervene in a complex and interdependent economy. A complex economy sometimes permits small groups of strategically placed workers to exert enormous influence over the functioning of the larger economy. The power of these strategic worker groups, such as longshoremen, teamsters, and some public employees, has helped accelerate the process of government intervention in labor conflict. As the structural transformation of the economy continues to produce groups of strategically located workers, we are likely to witness even more public intervention in a process which began with strictly private confrontations.

An Overview

The American labor movement has many unique features. Some derive from the historical circumstances in which American unionism emerged and developed, while other distinctly American features arise from the structure of the American economy. Chapter 2 surveys American labor history, highlighting the interdependency between the labor movement and the structure of the economy. Debates about the "proper" role and direction of the labor movement have a long tradition, and we discuss the struggles between those favoring economic and political union strategies, between craft and industrial unionists, and between groups within the labor movement. Since government has become such an important influence in labor relations, salient labor legislation and its impacts are described.

The 177 American trade unions have 20 million members in a labor force of 97 million persons, as described in Chapter 3. Although only one in five working persons is a union member, some industries, including steel and automobile production and the mining, contract construction, and transportation sectors, are highly organized. Employment is growing fastest in occupations without union traditions, especially in white-collar occupations. The growing importance of traditionally nonunion women and teenagers in the labor force, of sparsely organized white-collar workers, and the erosion of employment in traditional sectors of union strength portend future obstacles for union growth.

Resolving the fundamental clash among producer efficiency, worker security, and economic stability is the central theme of labor relations. The variety of·institutions for settling labor conflict and the historical circumstances which produced each are the subject of Chapter 4. Basic questions are posed: Why do workers join unions? Why do unions in some countries use political tactics rather than collective bargaining to achieve their goals? Is there a natural evolution of trade unionism that depends on economic growth? By exploring comparative labor theory, we can gain an appreciation of the variety of ways in which labor conflict can be resolved.

Unions differ from their management counterparts in several important ways. Both organizations are hierarchical, but business is organized to allow power to flow from top to bottom, while unions are organized as political institutions, with leaders subject to periodic elections. Unions function as representative democracies, with **locals** acting as the building blocks of national unions. Most of the important national unions are affiliated with the American Federation of Labor-Congress of Industrial Organizations, the AFL-CIO. Chapter 5 surveys those differences in structure that have important implications for the strategies adopted by unions and management in collective bargaining.

Collective bargaining, the subject of Chapter 6, is the heart of labor relations. Collective bargaining has two distinct phases: (1) negotiation of a collective bargaining agreement or contract, and (2) the administration of the resulting agreement. The negotiation phase, where conflicting *interests* are resolved, receives most public attention because of the strikes and **lockouts** that sometimes result from a failure to agree.

Bargaining strategies and tactics are the product of economic, political, and legal factors, causing relative union and management bargaining power to vary over time and across countries. The end result of bargaining ploys and tactics is a collective bargaining agreement, specifying wages and employment conditions for a one- to three-year period. Collective bargaining has proven to be a flexible instrument for resolving labor conflict. Despite the additional demands made upon it (as, for example, when a third party like the public interest demands representation to assure equal employment opportunity or ensure that the agreement coincides with national economic policy), collective bargaining appears flexible enough to accommodate both its traditional and its expanded role in labor relations.

The American labor relations system is governed by both public and private legal frameworks, combining to create a system of industrial jurisprudence. The public regulative framework is the body of labor relations law, enacted, amended, and interpreted, which defines the rights and duties of individuals, unions, and employers. The public framework is supplemented by a body of private law and procedure, the grievance mechanism for resolving *rights* granted by the collective bargaining agreement. Disputes over contract-generated rights, which occur during daily interaction between employees and supervisors, are usually appealed through a defined series of steps culminating in binding **arbitration,** or resolution of the dispute by a neutral third party. The public and private regulative frameworks are complementary—the public framework is largely responsible for governing election and negotiation procedures while the private framework serves to interpret an existing agreement by settling grievances arising under the agreement.

Union activity in the 1960s and 1970s has been heavily influenced by public sector organization and bargaining, the subject of Chapter 8. Between 1960 and 1975, public employment nearly doubled, and public sector union membership rose from insignificance to 3 million. Public sector unionism has had multiple causes and promises as yet ambiguous consequences, especially at state and local levels of government, where 80 percent of all public employees are located. At the state and local levels, the regulative framework varies, producing a wide variety of public sector labor relationships. As in many other industrial nations, American unions have organized a much higher proportion of the public labor force than the private.

The relative newness of labor institutions and their even shorter existence as legal entities leaves their current role unclear. Are unions too powerful or not powerful enough? Should unions confine their interest to workplace concerns or push for general social reforms? Should unions only react to management-initiated proposals or should they have a voice in formulating management policies? What are the implications of public sector unionism for (local) government democracy? Although an array of convictions on these issues exists, we can explore them in a manner which allows us to weigh the advantages and disadvantages of each.

Before concluding that unions or particular business or union tactics are repugnant, we should have a framework within which the worth of current labor institutions can be judged. One such test of social utility is by comparison, that is, what alternative institutions could resolve the conflicts arising in employment and production? Alternative mechanisms for resolving labor conflict—including relying on individuals who are dissatisfied to change employments, assuming that employers are benevolent, or allowing government regulations to assure workplace equity—have been proposed. Before accepting or rejecting the current framework for resolving labor conflict and promoting labor cooperation, we must understand the labor market and social functions union and management negotiators perform. Only then is an intelligent assessment of current labor relations possible.

The Evolution of American Unionism

2

The labor unions of the United States and Europe were spawned by groups of workers in craft shops even before the advent of the Industrial Revolution and factory production. Although craft unions antedate factory production, it was the "bringing together" of groups of workers in factories which finally resulted in mass union organization. The unions which emerged rarely enjoyed voluntary acceptance by employers. The employer, often an entrepreneur who had undertaken considerable risk in beginning a business, was reluctant to share decision-making authority in any area of management (including employment) with an upstart union. The result was an uneven, often violent struggle between labor and management. In labor's quest for legitimacy and acceptance of its proclaimed role of representative of the working man, basic questions had to be faced. Would unions pressure for acceptance in confrontations with employers, through legislative channels, or both? How should unions organize workers—in one big union, one union for each industry, or one union for each craft or worker skill? After unions secured a foothold, government was willing to intervene and erect a framework for union-management interaction. Now another set of issues had to be resolved. What rules were fair and equitable to both sides as well as to the public interest? As we shall see, this last issue remains prominent today.

The Craft Origins of Labor Unions

The earliest labor organizations were guilds in which both merchants and accomplished craftsmen (journeymen) met to discuss the apprenticeship rules regulating entry into the craft and to establish common prices and quality standards for the goods produced. Over time, the guilds came to assume mutual-aid functions, supporting a member or his widow in the event of disability or death. With the advent of the Industrial Revolution in eighteenth-century Europe and increased trade, both between town and country and among nations, these guilds were subject to competitive pressures from distant producers who cut prices and reduced product quality. The gap between the merchant-journeyman and his fellows increased. Journeymen in each craft (carpenters, shoemakers, hatters, and so on) formed unions to regulate apprenticeship and to ensure common prices when trading their goods—that is, trade unions. Among the labor force of the period, consisting of the self-employed nobility and royalty, merchants and craftsmen, a few nonfarm laborers, and the mass of farmworkers (peasants), these accomplished craftsmen were clearly the most privileged segment of the dependent work force.

In America, the early craft unions arose to counter the growing power of "middlemen," the merchant-capitalists who bought the craftsmen's products for later sale to customers. Before the emergence of the merchant-capitalist, each artisan had produced and sold his own products. Population growth, market expansion, and technological change resulted in a new class of entrepreneur, one who bought goods, assumed some risk by storing and transporting them, and sold them in both local and distant markets. The individual craftsman was reduced to production for an impersonal market, that is, for customers he never saw.

Competition among merchant-capitalists in turn generated competition among craftsmen. Rather than a single craftsman's producing the whole product, journeymen began using cheaper apprentice labor, with each apprentice producing only a part of the product (e.g., a shoe sole or heel), thus threatening to "dilute" the craft. The resulting downward pressure on craftsmen's wages led to the formation of unions which would assure a minimum price for the product of the craft, a price which was the wage of the journeyman who produced the whole thing. In 1792, the Philadelphia cordwainers (shoemakers) formed a local union to ward off the "competitive menace" of the middlemen.

Other local unions arose and disappeared but, in 1827, extant local craft unions united in the Mechanics Union of Trade Associations to fight for the ten-hour day. The 1827 date was pinpointed by John R. Commons, an eminent labor historian, to mark the founding of the American labor movement.

Not every trade union emerged from the market-induced break-up of guilds. In their survey of the emergence of unions, Sidney and Beatrice Webb found that craft unions did not spring "from any particular institution, but from every opportunity for the meeting together of wage earners of the same occupation."[1] In some instances, labor organizations arose with after-work fraternizing and drinking, while in other cases, unions emerged from demonstrations against public policies regulating maximum wages. Although unionism required a work force dependent on an employer for wages, it is important to remember that unions arose *before* the advent of factory production.

The early trade unions were subject to membership ebb and flow. Economic downturns resulted in mass membership losses, and employers successfully fought the fledgling unions in court. Between 1816 and 1819, for example, manufacturing employment is estimated to have decreased by over 75 percent.[2] Although only about 5 percent of the labor force was engaged in

---

[1]S. and B. Webb, *The History of Trade Unionism* (New York: Longman's, 1935), p. 10.

[2]Cited in S. Lebergott, "The Pattern of Employment since 1800," in S. Harris (ed.), *American Economic History* (New York: McGraw-Hill, 1961), p. 294.

manufacturing, such sharp economic downturns wreaked havoc on the fledgling unions by establishing a pool of unemployed workers eager for employment. If a union attempted to disrupt production, employers were quick to obtain injunctions to enjoin and fine strikers. In 1806, the legal position of labor unions was defined and summarized as: ". . . a combination of workmen to raise their wages must be considered from a two-fold point of view; one is to benefit themselves, the other to injure those who do not join their society. The rule of law condemns both."[3] It was not until 1842 that this "criminal conspiracy" view of unionism was reversed.

Despite an unfavorable economic and legal milieu, some important concessions were won by early craft unions. Limited success was achieved by the citywide federations of craft unions, especially in New York. Forming working-men's parties, they succeeded in winning general acceptance of the concepts of free public education and universal suffrage, rights which were to have important impacts on subsequent economic and social history. Even legal relief appeared. In 1842, the Massachusetts Supreme Court held that unions were to be judged by the *purposes* of their actions, not their actions in isolation. Unions could no longer be prosecuted as criminal conspiracies; it was now the duty of an employer to prove ill-purpose and seek monetary compensation.

Politics versus Economics, 1830–1886

The period from 1830 to 1886 was characterized by the struggle to establish the focus of trade union activity—would gains be sought in the economic sphere via collective bargaining or in politics with a labor party? Until the establishment of the Knights of Labor, the thrust of craft union activity had combined economics and politics—the craftsmen were the "aristocracy" of the labor force and had more economic power than the mass of unskilled workers. The Knights, founded in the 1860s by Uriah Stephens, sought societal harmony with the establishment of producer cooperatives and the abolition of the wage system. As a unity-seeking movement, it encouraged everyone to join, employers and workers alike (only "social parasites"—gamblers, bankers, stockbrokers, lawyers, and bartenders—were excluded).

The Knights reached their apex in 1886, when their 700,000 members represented 4 percent of the labor force. In 1886, two events occurred which ensured the demise of the Knights. On May 1, 1886, several demonstrators (including some anarchists) calling for the establishment of the eight-hour day were shot and killed by Chicago police. Three days later, on May 4, a protest against the police action was held in Haymarket Square. The protest ended with

---

[3]Philadelphia Cordwainers' Case [*Commonwealth* v. *Pullis*], Philadelphia Mayor's Court (1806). For a discussion of this case, see S. Nelles, "The First American Labor Case," *Yale Law Journal*, 41 (1931): 165. Note that only labor conspiracy is proscribed. In this pre-antitrust era, (owners of) capital could combine in order to increase profits.

the throwing of a bomb among a group of policemen, killing several. Severe repression followed (later research has established that the bomb was probably thrown by a police informer). The Haymarket incident, marking the turning point in the Knights' influence, is the origin of Labor Day celebrations, observed on May 1 in most countries.

Despite an effective existence of less than twenty years, the Knights of Labor exerted an important influence on the evolution of American unionism. Their political focus, which sought to lift wage earners from the laboring class, represented American labor's last serious fling with "the more romantic, reformist type of unionism," which became, in Perlman's metaphor, ". . . mere sieves into which membership poured only to pour out again."[4] The unions which followed would downgrade demands for producer cooperatives, income and inheritance taxes, nationalization of the railroads, and land taxation for pragmatic "business unionism," closely tied to workplace problems.

The American Federation of Labor (AFL)

The year 1886 also saw the founding of the American Federation of Labor (AFL) to counter the Knights among craftsmen. As a federation of national craft unions, the establishment of the AFL marked a new turn in the American labor movement. In the Civil War period, some twenty-six national unions had been founded. These nationals (or internationals, since they also had Canadian locals) were organized by combining local unions in each craft by trade (e.g., all carpenters in one union) rather than geography, as in the Philadelphia association of 1827. The national organizations soon gained control over their constituent locals. The national was responsible for collecting and disbursing strike funds, and exercised authority over local actions with its power to withhold strike funds. The national union, expanding with product markets, was responsible for organizing new workers and, as it assumed mutual insurance and benefit roles, the national union became the central clearinghouse for collecting such funds and disbursing them. The dominance of the national was assured by the economic bent of American craft unionism; had craft unionism centered on political bargaining, the locus of power could have been based on geographical units, since political officials are elected from such units. But the economic focus called for a continuing national body which could parallel the structure of the industry. As markets and industries expanded, so did trade unions.

Although economic bargaining dominated the outlook of individual nationals, the AFL *could* have assumed a more political role. But under Samuel Gompers, the AFL embraced a very restrictive view of the trade union func-

---

[4]S. Perlman and P. Taft, *History of Labor in the United States: 1896–1932* (New York: Macmillan, 1935), p. 5.

tion, epitomized by the demand for "more, now." Rather than promising utopia for all workers, the AFL offered economic assistance to the skilled "cream" of the labor force, explicitly eschewing organized political activities (such as labor parties) except for a limited "reward friends and punish enemies" policy. Compared with European labor movements in this period, the AFL was ideologically conservative, a circumstance which reflected: (1) the absence of strong religious or ideological convictions among (craft) union leaders; (2) the relative scarcity of labor in America, which permitted unions to win economic gains more easily than their European counterparts; and (3) the federal-state structure in America, which required political victories at two levels of government rather than merely at the federal level, as in Europe.

The political conservatism and reformist character of the early AFL reflected both ideological conviction and American reality. As a movement whose tactics were routinely declared illegal, the American labor movement needed "the support of public opinion . . . any suspicion that labor might harbor a design to do away altogether with private property, rather than merely regulating its use, immediately threw the public into an alliance with the anti-union employers."[5] In contrast to current political actions, this "minority consciousness" impelled the AFL to adopt an antigovernment position, often demonstrated by opposition to protective labor laws for regulating the hours and working conditions of women and children.

The political conservatism and economic bent of the AFL was reflected in the Federation's attitude toward immigrants. Immigrants were first opposed by the Knights of Labor. Subsequently, the AFL embarked on several campaigns, some with racist overtones, to restrict immigration. Immigrants, separated by language and culture, were often used as strikebreakers. Union pressures for the closed shop, under which the employer may hire only union members, emerged, in part, to permit union regulation of the labor supply. The "union label," first used to distinguish union from Chinese-made textiles in San Francisco, became a device for protecting existing jobs and unions. Although immigrants often became ardent unionists, the general AFL position found them to be "competitive menaces," to be controlled rather than abetted.

Despite the conservative stance of American unionism, the willingness of American unions to exert their economic power led businessmen to fight rather than accept organization. At the turn of the century, the National Association of Manufacturers (NAM) was founded to espouse the principle of unfettered management rights. Although the AFL was willing to concede that management had property rights in its machinery and factories, allowing them to stand idle if it so desired, the AFL insisted that if the plant operated, the union had to have a voice in the rules and regulations governing plant operation. Most businessmen were unwilling to concede a distinction between machinery in isolation and machinery with workers, preferring to assert that: "We will not permit

---

[5]Ibid., p. 5.

employees to place any restriction on the management, methods, or production of our shops.'' The battle lines were drawn.

The early 1900s were a period of industrial unrest. Management often exercised its ''right'' to fire an employee at whim, and supplemented this approach to discouraging union activity by maintaining ''blacklists'' of known union sympathizers. So-called **yellow-dog contracts,** which made continued employment contingent on remaining outside any union, were instituted. Disputes were accentuated by employers' refusal to recognize unions, even unions which had organized *all* workers in a plant, leading to numerous strikes for recognition. In addition, many coal, steel, and mining plants were effectively ''company towns,'' in which the employer owned local housing and services. In the event of strikes, violence often flared as local police forces, under the control of employers, attempted to evict strikers from company-owned housing. The Pinkerton Company became legendary for providing industrial spies and private security forces to quell labor protest.

The war years (1914–1918) proved beneficial to organized labor. The withdrawal of some men for military service increased the demand for those remaining, strengthening labor's bargaining position. A National War Labor Board was established to encourage the settlement of labor disputes. Although the Board had no formal powers of enforcement, it accorded organized labor a legitimacy in the war effort it had lacked in peacetime. The AFL flourished, surpassing the 4-million-member mark in 1920.

The postwar years revived antiunion activity. Bolstered by the scientific management school, management began to argue that unions not only usurped rights, they also hindered productive efficiency. Management argued that conditions of work should be established by (management-hired) ''experts,'' who would determine expected performances through time-and-motion studies and set wages according to ''objectively measured'' contribution-to-output indicators. Business began to concede the right of employees to some form of representation but held that this representation was best achieved on a company-by-company basis, not by allowing industrywide trade unions. The National Association of Manufacturers encouraged the founding of employee-representation plans, designed to supplant the union function by establishing a forum to settle local grievances. These representation plans, often decried as ''company unions,'' were supplemented by attacks on the loyalty of American union leaders in an era of concern for communists after the Russian Revolution of 1917. Organized labor had not yet established its legitimacy in America.

The 1920s marked the last ebb of the AFL. Membership declined throughout the 1920s, and by 1933 was only one half its 1920 level. Employer opposition, the Depression, and AFL organizing principles were jointly responsible for the decrease. The AFL, founded by craft union leaders, organized workers primarily by trade, not industry. Thus, in an auto plant, the AFL would charter one union for machinists, one for carpenters, and so on. Although the AFL attempted organization in such industries with a single organizing committee, it expected to parcel out the workers among their various crafts once a plant was organized.

This craft basis of organization suffered serious defects. Dividing the labor force along craft lines could make unity more difficult to achieve, especially in large factories where different groups of workers would be represented by separate unions. More important, craftsmen reflect the skills existing at a point in time. With economic development, new skills are created, especially in the dynamic, expanding industries. While competing craft unions must first decide who has jurisdiction over new skills, the established industrial union naturally includes any such workers. In a dynamic economy, the industrial union is usually better situated to organize workers with the new skills which emerge in a particular industry.[6]

Before turning to the rise of mass industrial unionism under John L. Lewis and the Congress of Industrial Organizations (CIO), we should mention the competition to craft unionism provided by continuing "radical" trade unions. Their lack of success in America often distorts retrospective analyses. The Industrial Workers of the World (IWW), or "Wobblies," represented one of the more colorful radical organizations, and its experiences are indicative of the difficulties faced by any nontraditional organization attempting to assist a group of workers. The IWW, founded in 1905, organized low-wage workers in several sectors, notably migrant agricultural labor and lumberjacks. Employer opposition was fierce. The wages paid were very low, never allowing the union to collect regular dues and enjoy financial health. The IWW, which did not recognize the legitimacy of employers, refused to sign contracts, allowing the employer to retract promises made in the heat of strikes and lockouts. Because it opposed U.S. entry into World War I, the IWW was subject to investigations by the federal government, and the internal divisions generated led to its demise after World War I. Thus, because they focused on the "worst off" rather than the skilled aristocracy of the labor force and because they sought to *replace* the employer rather than merely modify his actions in bargaining, the more radical organizing efforts operated under much more serious handicaps than the mainstream labor movement.

The Rise of the Congress of Industrial Organizations (CIO)

As noted, the craft basis of organization left the AFL ill equipped to organize the growing sector of the work force, factory or industrial workers in basic manufacturing industries (steel, auto, and so on). John L. Lewis, head of the United Mine Workers within the AFL, sought to foster organization among industrial workers by creating an unofficial "Committee for Industrial Organization" in 1935. Lewis aimed to organize the industrial labor force by enrolling

---

[6]In economic sectors where crafts are well established, even a change in the necessary skills may not threaten a craft union. In the public sector, most workers are organized along craft lines. Even if the skills necessary for teaching, police work, or firefighting change, the craft unions of teachers, policemen, or firefighters will not be seriously threatened.

all workers in a plant into a single union. This action, which ran counter to the established AFL policy of permitting separate unions of skilled craftsmen and industrial workers, led to Lewis's expulsion and the creation of the Congress of Industrial Organizations (CIO) in 1938. The Depression, the inability of government to restore prosperity, and the tendency for wage cutting among employers had led to an undercurrent of receptiveness to unionization among industrial workers, and the regularization of election procedures provided by the Wagner Act (1935) allowed union membership to explode. Representing only 3 million workers in 1933, organized labor expanded to include 9 million by 1939, one third of the labor force.

Union organizing efforts in the 1930s were often marked by violence. Some employers believed unions to be morally wrong, holding that pressures for organization resulted only because of "outside agitation." In 1914, George Baer, a railroad and coal magnate, typified this attitude with his infamous statement: "The rights and interests of the laboring man will be protected and cared for not by labor agitators but by Christian men to whom God, in his infinite wisdom, has given control of the property interests of the country." This continuing refusal to recognize unions led to a rash of strikes for recognition, some 2,400 in 1937 alone.

Some employers accepted unionism after the workers staged **sitdown strikes.** These strikes, during which the workers remained at their machines (to prevent **scab** production) were successful in organizing the automobile and rubber companies. Other companies routinely used strikebreakers and private security forces to discourage unionization. In coal mining, for example, such employer actions produced widespread violence. In one notorious case, the Harlan County (Kentucky) Coal Operators Association paid the salaries of 160 of the 163 deputy sheriffs in the county. The deputies, in turn, assumed responsibility for harassing and sometimes killing union organizers as well as encouraging and protecting strikebreakers. Not until the newly established National Labor Relations Board ruled against the mine operators in 1938 was labor peace restored. For many employers, only legal compulsion could force recognition of a labor union.

The Legal Framework

The period of explosive growth in the thirties was aided by the establishment of a framework for organizing and bargaining, a framework which survives to this day. Before the 1930s, there had been no explicit legal framework governing employer-employee relations. Under **common** (judge-made) **law,** private property rights were broadly construed. Employers were given a relatively free hand to hire and fire; to determine hours and conditions of work (maximum hours for women and children were legislatively established during World War I); and to refuse to recognize any employee organization. By the mid-nineteenth century, unions were no longer prosecuted (by public prosecutors) as criminal conspiracies, but employers could still seek to halt or enjoin union actions.

In 1877, the union movement received a setback with the "invention" of the labor **injunction.** Injunctions, writs (orders) of a court which are issued at the behest of *one* party and require or proscribe certain actions, had traditionally been employed to uphold the court's own authority. Workers on a bankrupt railroad being operated by court-appointed trustees went on strike, so the trustees sought an injunction to end the strike action.

If the labor injunction had been confined to court trusteeships, it would not have evolved into its role as the continuing "menace to the right to strike" in American labor history. But the courts held that the public interest was affected in both financially sound and in bankruptcy situations, and the labor injunction was extended, first to other railroads, then to all business firms. If a union threatened a strike, the employer could now obtain an injunction prohibiting the threatened action. If the union struck anyway, *public authorities,* rather than the employer's agents, would deal with the strikers.

Until the 1930s, common (judge-made) law tended to hamstring union activities. But **statutory law** (legislation) was no less antiunion. Employers obtained injunctions by arguing that they were protecting the public from rapacious unions, unions who would jack up costs and thus prices to the consuming public. It was not until 1890 that Congress recognized the power of the large business firm to increase prices independent of union pressures. Passage of the Sherman Anti-Trust Act (1890) made it more difficult for businesses to hide behind the cloak of mere intermediaries between unions and the public, pretending to increase prices only because of union-generated cost increases.

The Sherman Act, which permitted the collection of treble damages in the event of actions which were in "restraint of trade," was construed to cover union activities as well. In the Danbury Hatters case, tried in 1908 and again in 1915, the Supreme Court held that attempts by striking hatters in Danbury, Connecticut, to institute a nationwide **boycott** against the hats made by a nonunion hatmaker were a restraint on interstate commerce. The union (and its members) were held liable for $210,000, a sum obtained only after AFL appeals. In addition to limiting the usefulness of the organized boycott, the Sherman Act constrained union strike activity. In *Coronado Coal Company* v. *United Mine Workers,* tried in 1922 and 1925, the Supreme Court held that, if the *purpose* of a strike was to prevent the interstate movement of goods (in this case, coal which was already mined), the strike was illegal under the Sherman Act. If, on the other hand, the interstate flow of goods was halted as a by-product of a strike whose *intent* was not to disrupt trade, the strike action was legal.

Until the 1930s, the burden of both common and statutory law had been to restrict union activities by narrowly defining permissible union tactics. Despite these legal constraints, the AFL experienced slow but steady growth. The ability of unions to recruit members, gain recognition, and obtain agreements in the face of such odds testifies to a real need for workplace representation. This need for representation was also recognized by employers. At President Wilson's National Labor-Management Conference in 1918, some employers agreed that unions were necessary but held that each union must be confined to the employees of a single company, since unions with employees in several companies could play one employer off against another.

This changing attitude toward unions, according them a legitimate representation role in an economy dominated by large business firms, evolved in an era when America was receptive to fundamental changes. The inability to end the Depression swept Franklin D. Roosevelt to power with a mandate to restore economic prosperity. The Wagner Act declared that "the inequality of bargaining power between employees. . . and employers . . . tends to aggravate recurrent business depressions, by depressing wage rates and the purchasing power of wage earners." The federal government assumed a new posture—it now *encouraged* organization and collective bargaining as a means to ensure both labor peace and restore economic prosperity. The Wagner Act era had arrived.

The Wagner Act was not without precedent. In 1926, the politically powerful railroad unions had secured passage of the Railway Labor Act, providing railroad workers organization rights nine years before these rights were obtained by the industrial labor force. The Norris-LaGuardia Act of 1932 outlawed yellow-dog contracts and curtailed the ability of federal courts to enjoin union **picketing** activities by issuing **cease-and-desist orders.** But the new attitude was first embodied in Section 7(a) of the National Industrial Recovery Act (1933), which granted general legal protection to workers and unions. Declared unconstitutional by the Supreme Court, the NIRA was superseded by the National Labor Relations Act (NLRA) of 1935, known as the Wagner Act for the New York senator who introduced it.

Upheld by the Supreme Court in 1937, the NLRA sought to rationalize labor-management relations by providing a legal framework, rules, and an appeals process to govern the interaction of unions and management. The federal government now encouraged collective bargaining by requiring unions and managements to meet and confer "in good faith." Although government could not force agreement, it could create conditions which made settlement more probable.

The Wagner Act defined the rights of workers, enumerated a series of employer **unfair** (unlawful) **labor practices (ULPs),** and created a National Labor Relations Board (NLRB) to supervise representative elections and hear unfair labor practice complaints. Under the theory that organization and union selection should be "neutral," workers are given rights (Section 7) to self-organization, to form, join, or assist labor organizations, and to bargain collectively through representatives of their own choosing, all without employer interference, coercion, or restraint. Additional employer unfair labor practices include employer domination or creation of unions and discrimination against workers to "chill" trade union activity. After the NLRB conducts an election to certify which, if any, union is to represent a group of workers, the employer is required to bargain "in good faith" with the union (and only with the certified union)[7] over wages, fringe benefits, work rules, and changes in plant operations, for example, subcontracting or (partial) shutdown. The NLRB, in addition to supervising and certifying unions as bargaining representatives, was created to act as a tribunal for hearing unfair labor practice charges, permitting the authority of government to intervene on the side of labor in cases where employers used unlawful tactics to forestall unionization.

The National Labor Relations Act, sometimes viewed as only a "by-product" of the overarching drive for economic recovery, remains the fundamental labor relations law in the United States. The NLRA only required **good-faith bargaining** with a union; it did not compel agreement. Although organization and certification procedures were now subject to legal constraints, collective bargaining was left to the largely private dealings between the union and management parties.

The war years (1941–1945) witnessed continued union growth. In exchange for labor cooperation (a no-strike pledge) in the war effort, the federal government pressed employers to recognize unions attempting organization. From 9 million members in 1940, the unionized labor force increased 67 percent to 15 million by 1950. But the postwar period produced a rash of strikes, as unions sought to outdistance price increases and reassert their strike power after the war period's quiescence. The feeling that the NLRA had yielded "too much" to organized labor led to demands for legislation to check union power, culminating in the Taft-Hartley Act (1947). The Taft-Hartley Act imposed many of the same constraints on unions which the NLRA had imposed on management—it recognized that both management *and* unions could commit unfair labor practices; it provided for elections both to certify and *decertify* a union; it established procedures to deal with "national emergency" strikes; and it permitted **state right-to-work laws,** allowing states to pass legislation which prohibited the negotiation of agreements making union membership a condition for continued employment (i.e., the union shop).

During World War II, a series of labor-management boards were created to ensure strike-free production of war material. In some instances, the labor policies pioneered by these boards have had lasting impacts on American labor relations. The National War Labor Board, for example, was responsible for settling labor disputes, and the Board fulfilled its charge by ordering the inclusion of arbitration clauses in new contracts when the parties were unable to select a method for settling grievances. The idea of using outside (neutral) arbitrators to decide what the contract "really means" in the day-to-day disputes which arise while an agreement is in force was an important innovation, since it allowed work to continue but assured both the aggrieved worker(s) and management "justice" despite the postponement of a decision on the issue. In

---

[7]Once a union is certified, it obtains *exclusive* jurisdiction over a group of workers. After certification, all employer actions related to wages and conditions of employment must be by mutual consent; for example, the employer is *not* allowed to offer the workers a Christmas bonus without consultation with the union.

the early 1930s, arbitration of grievances was limited to about 10 percent of all labor agreements; by 1944, nearly three fourths of all agreements contained arbitration clauses.[8]

By the early 1950s, trade union growth had slowed. After the expulsion of alleged communists in certain CIO unions and the retirement of several rivals in the separate federations, the way to a merger of the two federations was paved. The rival federations were merged into the AFL-CIO in 1955, a total of 139 separate unions representing 16 million workers, one fourth of the U.S. labor force. The dispute between those who believed that workers should be organized by craft (AFL) versus those who believed in industrywide organization (CIO) ended by allowing established patterns of organization to persist, with the AFL-CIO acting as arbiter in jurisdictional disputes between member unions.

Constraints on organized labor did not end with the passage of the Taft-Hartley Act. During 1957 and 1958, Congressional exposure of widespread racketeering in several national unions, notably the Teamsters, led to renewed calls for reform. Following the initial exposure, the Teamsters were expelled from the AFL-CIO in 1957 and the Congressional hearings produced the Landrum-Griffin Act (1959), which sought to provide union members with a "Bill of Rights" on union leadership and mandated regular disclosure of union finances.

New trends in private sector bargaining in the 1950s and 1960s influenced both the content of agreements and the handling of grievances. New pension, health, and supplemental unemployment benefits became the basis for a union-initiated private social security system, financed by worker and employer contributions rather than tax revenues. Threats of wholesale labor displacement with rapid automation placed new strains on collective bargaining but demonstrated that collective bargaining can be an effective means for dealing with technological change. Finally, the 1960s witnessed the expansion of grievance arbitration, first given widespread use during World War II. Now embraced by both unions and management, arbitration of grievances has been recognized as a major contributor to labor peace.

Contemporary Unionism

By 1960, union members represented 22.6 percent of the labor force, a 1 percent decrease from 1955 and a sharp drop from the high-water mark of the late thirties, when unions represented one in three workers. Between 1960 and 1976, trade unions gained about 2 million members, but a more rapidly growing labor force deceased the union share from 22.6 to 20 percent of all workers. As we shall see, trade union growth was slowed because of the *direction* of

---

[8]Cited in S. Slichter, J. Healy, and E. Livernash, *The Impact of Collective Bargaining on Management* (Washington, D.C.: The Brookings Institution, 1960), p. 739.

labor force growth—in areas where unions were well established (manufacturing, transportation, mining, and others), total employment failed to grow or contracted. Employment in white-collar occupations and the service sector expanded, but the dearth of established unions in these sectors impeded organization. In addition to a changing economic structure, the limited expansions which did occur in sectors of traditional union strength (e.g., manufacturing) often appeared in areas of low union proneness, the South and rural areas in America.[9]

Two sectors experienced union growth in the 1960s—public sector (white-collar) employees and low-wage workers in both the public and private sectors. Under two Executive Orders in 1962, President Kennedy permitted the organization of federal employees in all federal agencies except those involving national security. The Executive Orders guarantee federal employees the right to join unions and grant exclusive jurisdiction (one union per employee group) to labor organizations winning a majority vote in recognition elections where at least 60 percent of the eligible employees vote. Unions granted exclusive jurisdiction can negotiate agreements (although the scope of any agreement which can be negotiated is limited) and can establish a grievance procedure. Opposition to federal unions among some agency managements has confined union activity to federal departments with the most employees, notably the Postal Service, the Defense Department, and employees of the Department of Health, Education, and Welfare (HEW).

State and local government employees, constituting nearly 80 percent of total government payrolls, exhibit a more uneven pattern of organization. In this nonfederal public sector, organization appears directly related to jurisdictional size, that is, almost all cities of more than 1 million have municipal unions of policemen, firefighters, teachers, and so on, but the degree of organization drops erratically as city size decreases. The most important single group of public employees are teachers, who often represent one fourth of a local government's total employment. Since state and local government payrolls are the most rapidly expanding sectors of public employment, the success of organizing drives among these groups will largely determine the shape of public sector unionism.

The other area of significant union expansion has been among low-wage workers in the public, nonprofit, and private sectors. We have noted that, historically, unionism began with the labor aristocracy, only undertaking the organization of the mass of unskilled laborers in the 1930s. Low-paid workers were neglected even longer—it was not until the 1960s that sustained organizing drives were mounted. In many respects, the low-paid are most susceptible to organization but most difficult to organize—while low wages and inferior

---

[9]A prime example of these employment shifts is the postwar movement of textile dyeing and finishing plants from the Northeast to the Southeast. In 1946, about 30 percent of the textile work force was in the Southeast; by 1976, the southeastern states contained over two thirds of all textile workers. The southeastern textile industry has been among the most difficult for unions to organize.

working conditions generate a concern for change, low-wage industries tend to be low-profit, competitive ones, making employers unwilling to accept unions because individual employers *could* not grant wage increases and remain competitive. The low-wage labor force typically contains those with less education, little aggressiveness, and few leadership skills. Since organized labor long ". . . assumed that a labor group that needed outside aid to give it the original impulse to assert its independence (i.e., organize) was something of a questionable addition to the family of organized labor,"[10] neglect had been institutionalized.

Organization among the low-wage labor force was fostered by several forces which coalesced in the 1960s. The demonstration effect of the civil rights marches promoted a sense of self-respect and provided experience in group action, encouraging ethnic-based group actions to gain economic ends (for example, Cesar Chavez and the United Farm Workers). More significantly, the large proportion of low-wage workers employed in the public and nonprofit sectors encouraged organization; as teachers, firemen, and policemen organized, so did sanitation workers, nurses and nurses' aides, maintenance personnel, and others. One effect of these successful organizing drives has been to reduce the remaining pool of low-wage workers, thus artificially lowering the rate of apparent organizing success in this sector as the wages of newly organized workers rise. In the next chapter, we examine trends in the labor force in more detail, seeking to discern those shifts which can help predict future areas of union growth.

Summary

Unions arose among skilled craftsmen in America when market expansion and technological change produced capitalist middlemen, more interested in price and quantity than the quality of the craftsman's product. To counter competition, craftsmen formed "trade" unions to preserve common prices in trade.

Until 1886, American unionism floundered. Some national unions, such as the Knights of Labor, gained and lost members in roller-coaster fashion. In 1886, the American Federation of Labor (AFL), an association of national craft unions, established the principles of American business unionism. The AFL philosophy, which limited union goals to job control (rather than worker's control) and organized workers along craft lines, was challenged by the Congress of Industrial Organizations (CIO) in 1935. The two federations competed with one another until their merger as the AFL-CIO in 1955.

The 1930s represent the high-water mark of unionism in America. The Depression, distrust of big business, and an activist, interventionist government set the stage for a tripling of union membership. A legal framework which

---

[10]Perlman and Taft, *History of Labor in the U.S.,* p. 9.

committed government to favor unions and collective bargaining was established by the Wagner Act of 1935, lifting a legacy of legislative and judicial restraints on union activity. Union power was curbed in 1947 and again in 1959, but the basic legal framework remained intact.

By the 1960s, trade union growth had slowed. In 1962, the federal government issued orders encouraging organization among federal white-collar employees, and a new round of membership growth ensued. Union membership in federal, state, and local government blossomed, among both white-collar workers and those working in such traditionally low-paying occupations as nursing and sanitation. In the 1970s, white-collar workers, public employees, and lower-paid persons in the service sector promise to be the reservoirs from which new union members are drawn.

Bibliography

Commons, J., et al. *History of Labor in the United States*. New York: Macmillan, 1918. Four volumes.

The definitive history of the emergence of unions in America and their development through the nineteenth century.

Pelling, H. *A Short History of the American Labor Movement*. Chicago: University of Chicago Press, 1969.

A well-written history.

Taft, Philip. *Organized Labor in American History*. New York: Harper & Row, 1964.

The *magnum opus* of America's leading labor historian.

Ulman, L. *The Rise of the National Trade Union*. Cambridge, Mass.: Harvard University Press, 1955.

A detailed study of union expansion.

U.S. Department of Labor. *Brief History of the American Labor Movement*. Washington, D.C.: U.S. Government Printing Office, 1976.

A good summary with a valuable chronology.

Unions in the Labor Force

Unions are worker organizations which negotiate wages and conditions of employment for the labor force each represents. How many potential union members are there? How are actual union members distributed across industries and occupations? How does the American labor movement differ from unions in other countries? In this chapter, the size, composition, and deployment of the American labor force is described. The unions that organize this labor force usually operate in specific jurisdictions (e.g., one or more industries or crafts). In contrast to labor movements elsewhere, the 20 percent of the American labor force in unions is relatively low. Changes in union membership reflect changes in both the number of potential union members in each jurisdiction as well as union organizing drives and employer countermeasures. Although it is necessary to make an excursion into data analysis here, our reward is a better understanding of the linkages between the structure of the economy and the labor movement.

The Labor Force

In 1976, the U.S. population totaled some 214.4 million persons. The civilian labor force (CLF), comprising those sixteen years and older who are employed or seeking work, included 94.8 million people—44.2 percent of the total population. Why does 44 percent of the population work to support the other 56 percent? The nonworking groups include children under sixteen (about 60 million in 1976) and nearly 23 million elderly, leaving only 132.1 million persons (61.6 percent of the population) in the prime working age group—those between sixteen and sixty-five. The three in ten persons of prime working age not in the CLF include those in the armed forces, students, housewives, the disabled, and discouraged workers.

The 94.8 million Americans in the CLF are both employed and unemployed but seeking work. In 1976, 87.5 million persons were employed and 7.3 million were unemployed. The unemployment rate is simply the ratio of the unemployed to the labor force; for example, in 1976, the unemployment rate was 7.7 percent. The unemployment rate is one indicator of the ability of an economy to provide jobs; it directly affects the size of the labor force since more people tend to seek work when more jobs are available.

The CLF is composed of 94.8 million individuals distributed across occupations and industries. Traditionally, men have dominated the labor force, contributing six of every ten employed and unemployed persons (56.4 million) to the 1976 labor force. Male attachment to the labor force is decreasing; more education and earlier retirements have reduced the proportion of all men sixteen and older who work or seek employment from 82.4 percent in 1960 to 76.4 percent in 1976. Although most men work for some period of their lives, the trend is to work fewer years by beginning work later and retiring earlier.

The decline in male labor force participation has been offset by increasing female labor force entry. In 1976, 47.2 percent of all women sixteen and older were in the labor force—up from 37.1 percent in 1960. Women now account for 40 percent of those in the labor force, a dramatic jump since World War II. Minority males tend to work less than white males, but proportionately more minority females work than their white counterparts. In 1976, the 10.9 million minority workers represented 11 percent of the labor force.

The CLF is distributed across occupations, with shifts between occupations reflecting underlying structural changes in the economy. Between 1960 and 1976, workers shifted from agricultural and blue-collar occupations to white-collar and service jobs, continuing a postwar trend (Figure 3.1). One in every two workers is now in a white-collar job, one in three still wears a blue collar, 13 percent are in service industries, and 3 percent are engaged in agriculture. Historically, male workers released from agriculture have taken blue-collar jobs—from which some later shifted into white-collar work—while women often enter the white-collar sector upon entry into the labor force. In 1976, 63 percent of all employed women were in white-collar jobs compared with 41 percent of employed males. Males are concentrated in blue-collar work (46 percent), while women are found more frequently in services (21 percent) than in blue-collar jobs (14 percent).

The CLF is also distributed across industries. In 1976, nonagricultural industries employed some 78 million wage and salary workers, an increase of 46 percent since 1960. Between 1965 and 1976, industry groups experienced employment changes which reflect shifts in demand and production. The slowest-growing industry sector was manufacturing, adding only 4.9 percent more workers and today accounting for fewer than one in four jobs.[1] Within the manufacturing group, nondurable manufacturing employment gained only 3.6 percent more employees, reflecting the halving of payrolls in just eleven years in cigar manufacturing and hat production as well as significant drops in textile, apparel, and leather employment. The fastest-growing industry group was services, adding one worker for every two employed in 1965. Other sectors experiencing above-average employment growth include wholesale and retail

---

[1] Employment change figures must be interpreted with caution because choice of comparison years can greatly influence apparent change. If comparisons were drawn between 1965 and 1975, which was a year of economic recession, manufacturing employment would have increased only 1.6 percent over the decade.

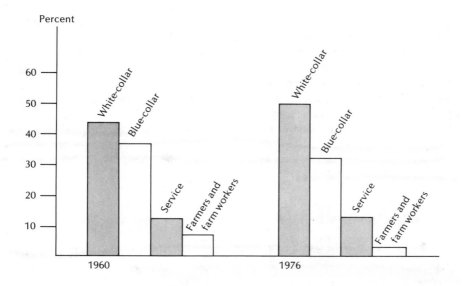

Percent

Figure 3.1. Labor Force Deployment, 1960 and 1976

Source: U.S. Department of Labor and U.S. Department of Health, Education and Welfare, *Employment and Training Report of the President* (Washington, D.C.: U.S. Government Printing Office, 1977).

trade (up 39.1 percent); finance, insurance, and real estate (up 42.7 percent); and government (up 48.4 percent). Thus, the shift from the production of goods to the provision of services is reflected in the trend toward white-collar employment in trade, government, and both financial and personal services.

As the economy evolves, structural changes will continue. Between 1974 and 1985, the total labor force is expected to grow slightly faster than the total population, increasing from 93 million to 111 million over the eleven-year period. Male attachment to the labor force is projected to stabilize with about three in four (76 percent) of all males sixteen years and older working or seeking employment in 1985. Female participation is expected to continue its upward spiral. By 1985, fully half of all females sixteen and older are expected to be in the labor force, increasing the female share of the total labor force from 40 percent to 42 percent in one decade.

The rising importance of working females is illustrated by occupational and industrial deployment projections. Total employment is expected to increase by 17 million or 20 percent between 1974 and 1985. Clerical occupations are projected to grow fastest (up 34 percent). Other rapidly expanding occupations include professional and technical workers (up 29.4 percent) and service workers (up 28 percent). Rapidly expanding occupations have included high proportions of women while slow-growing and declining occupations are male dominated. Operatives and nonfarm laborers are projected to expand only 9 percent—far less than the 20 percent employment expansion. The farm labor force is expected to continue shrinking (down 39 percent by 1985).

Projected industrial employment shifts parallel the occupational projections. The two sectors expected to increase their shares of total employment fastest, government and services, are expected to hire a high proportion of women. Traditional male sectors such as manufacturing and transport should decline in relative importance; by 1985, only one in four persons is expected to be employed in the production and transport sectors. The rise of the service economy is clear when it is realized that three industry sectors—government, services, and wholesale and retail trade—will employ more than 62 percent of the labor force by 1985.

Labor Unions: A Profile

Trends in both labor-force composition and the occupational and industrial deployment of working people affect union membership. In 1976, some 19.4 million persons belonged to 177 labor unions, representing 20.1 percent of the total labor force or 24.5 percent of the nonagricultural work force.[2] The labor force has expanded much more rapidly than has union membership, causing the unionized share of the labor force to decrease (Figure 3.2). Over the period between 1974 and 1976, both the number and share of union members in the labor force declined. The 16.6 million AFL-CIO unionists who comprise 80 percent of all union members are distributed across the 111 unions affiliated with the AFL-CIO (Figure 3.3). Labor's "minority image" is often derived from these statistics—the AFL-CIO is the certified labor "spokesperson" for fewer than one in five working persons.

In recent years, **employee associations** have assumed an increasing importance in labor relations. In 1976, the Department of Labor identified thirty-five professional and state employee associations, having some 3 million members. These self-named associations are considered labor organizations if they represent at least some members in collective negotiations with an employer and if the association has chapters in two or more cities within a state or two or more states. Almost all associations represent public employees, and the largest, the National Education Association (NEA), is the country's second largest labor organization, with 1.7 million members. The distinction between unions and associations is often blurred in labor relations; for example, both the American Federation of Teachers (an AFL-CIO union) and the NEA call strikes to press their bargaining demands.

Union membership varies across industries and occupations. Underground mining is the most unionized industry, having organized almost 90 percent of

---

[2]In addition to union members, another 3.1 million persons belonged to employee associations in 1976. These associations, containing largely white-collar workers (81 percent), are growing faster than labor unions. Over time, some of these associations assume union structures and functions, sometimes making their separation from the labor movement tenuous.

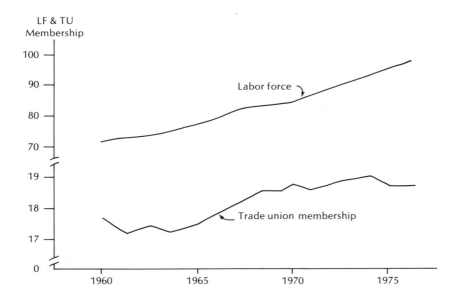

Figure 3.2. Trends in the Labor Force and Union Membership*

Source: U.S. Department of Labor, Bureau of Labor Statistics, *Directory of National Unions and Employee Associations, 1975* bulletin 1937 and supplements (Washington, D.C.: U.S. Government Printing Office, 1977).

*Excludes 3 million members of associations and 1.5 million Canadian union members.

its labor force. Other industries with more than 75 percent of the labor force in unions include transportation, contract construction, ordnance, paper, electrical machinery, and transportation equipment. These high rates of organization reflect both aggressive union leadership and peculiar industry features; for example, transportation workers derive their enormous bargaining power from both leadership and their strategic economic role, while ordnance workers are (indirectly) employed by the federal government, which favors organization and bargaining.

Many manufacturing industries have between 50 and 75 percent of their labor forces organized into unions. Although unions are often associated with factory production, it should be remembered that unions originated with skilled craftworkers and still command more loyalty outside manufacturing than in it. Other industries with more than half their labor forces in unions include petroleum (refining), food processing and distribution, communications (telephone and telegraph), and the federal government (if employee association membership is included).

Some industries have relatively few union members. Low rates of organization can result from the newness of organizing efforts, as in low-wage industries, or a past lack of effective legal tools and leadership, as in agriculture. Some employers have long resisted unions (e.g., textile mill operators and

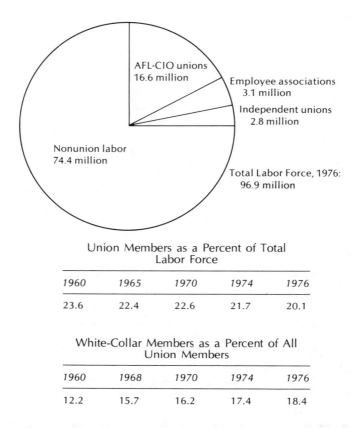

Union Members as a Percent of Total
Labor Force

1960	1965	1970	1974	1976
23.6	22.4	22.6	21.7	20.1

White-Collar Members as a Percent of All
Union Members

1960	1968	1970	1974	1976
12.2	15.7	16.2	17.4	18.4

Figure 3.3. Unions in the Labor Force, 1976

farmers), while others have adopted "union substitution" personnel policies, which provide rules and procedures for aggrieved employees to appeal workplace disputes. Low rates of organization are also present in industries with many small establishments, as in services, or in establishments with a high proportion of part-time workers, for example, wholesale and retail trade.

Organization rates across occupations mirror those in different industries. Operatives, the semiskilled workers who form the backbone of the blue-collar work force, are best organized, with nearly 63 percent in unions. Skilled craftsmen follow with a 50 percent organization rate. White-collar workers, including professionals, managers, salesworkers, and clerks, are much less organized. Clerical workers are the most organized white-collar group, with about 25 percent belonging to unions. Rates of union organization among service workers and farm workers are very low.

In addition to industrial and occupational differences, union organization rates vary across states. West Virginia and Michigan have the highest proportion of their work forces in unions (38 percent)—a reflection of the location of

Table 3.1. Membership in Selected Unions:
1966 and 1976

Union	Membership		Change (percent)
	1966	1976	1966–1976
Teamsters (Ind.)*	1,651,000	1,889,000	14.4
Automobile Workers (Ind.)*	1,403,000	1,358,000	(−3.2)
Steelworkers	1,068,000	1,300,000	21.7
Electrical (IBEW)	875,000	924,000	5.6
Machinists	836,000	917,000	9.7
Carpenters	800,000	820,000	2.5
Retail Clerks (RCIA)	500,000	699,000	39.8
Laborers (IUNA)	475,000	627,000	32.0
State, County (AFSCME)	281,000	750,000	166.9
Service Employees (SEIU)	349,000	575,000	64.7
Meat Cutters	353,000	510,000	44.5
Communications Workers	321,000	483,000	50.5
Teachers (AFTU)	125,000	446,000	256.8
Garment, Ladies (ILGWU)	455,000	365,000	(−19.8)
Government (AFGE)	200,000	260,000	30.0

Source: U.S. Department of Labor, Bureau of Labor Statistics, Directory of National Unions and Employee Associations, 1975 (Washington, D.C.: U.S. Government Printing Office, 1977).

*(Ind.) indicates that the union is independent of the AFL-CIO.

unionized coal mining and transportation equipment manufacturers. In eight other industrial states—New York, Pennsylvania, Ohio, Indiana, Illinois, Missouri, Washington, and Hawaii—more than one third of all nonagricultural employees are in unions. The southeastern states, long the bastion of antiunion traditions, have low rates of organization. North and South Carolina, with 7 and 8 percent organization, are the least organized states in the nation.

Just as union membership is concentrated among certain industries and occupations in several states, so are union members consolidated in the largest national unions (Table 3.1). The Teamsters union is the nation's largest, with almost 2 million members (9 percent of all unionized workers) in a wide variety of industries.[3] The United Auto Workers Union (UAW) is second largest, with over 1.5 million members in auto and agricultural implement production as well as aerospace and auto parts. Both the Teamsters and the UAW are outside the AFL-CIO. The largest AFL-CIO union is the United Steelworkers of America, with 1.3 million members.

Most union members are found in the large national unions. In 1974, the twelve largest unions contained 11.1 million members—over one half of all union members. Among the larger national unions, those organizing public employees have experienced the most rapid growth, doubling and sometimes tripling membership in just one decade. Unions active among low-wage workers, including the service employees and the retail clerks, experienced above-

---

[3]Union membership data are not trouble free. Some unions overreport membership (e.g., the Carpenter's Union) while others underreport. As long as individual unions maintain the same bias in reporting membership, at least the ten-year change indicator is accurate.

normal growth, as did the Communication Workers Union, which organizes workers in another expanding industry. More traditional unions, like the Teamsters and Auto Workers, have pursued vigorous organizing campaigns, helping to account for their membership gains.

What accounts for differential union growth? The most important determinants of changes in union size are changes in the pool of persons in the union's organizing jurisdiction. Public employment grew very rapidly in the 1960s and 1970s, a partial explanation for the dramatic rise in public employee union membership; but aggressive leadership and favorable public policies also helped. The federal government's decision to encourage public employee organization in 1962 was a spur to federal employee unions, just as the aggressive leadership of the American Federation of State, County, and Municipal Employees (AFSCME) helps explain its membership spurt. Sometimes leadership and public policy can offset employment trends. The United Farm Workers Union (UFW) was able to begin its rebirth during 1976 and 1977 after securing a legal framework in California and settling a jurisdictional dispute with competing Teamsters.

The rising importance of females in the labor force and white-collar workers in the economy has already been noted. Both groups of workers are underrepresented in American unions when compared to their importance in the labor force. The 4.2 million women in unions in 1976 were about 20 percent of all union members—a female union share that has remained relatively constant since 1960. But, over the same period, women have increased from less than one third of the labor force to comprise 40 percent of all workers. As the female share of the labor force continues to increase, the union share of the labor force will continue decreasing, unless more women are organized.

Why have women been so difficult to organize into labor unions? Opinions range the gamut from male chauvinist union leaders to assertions that female attachment to the labor force is too casual to encourage union receptivity. It is true that women are most frequently found in lower-level, white-collar occupations;[4] that the nature of such work, including small office pools with direct employer contact, impairs unionism; and that many women work only part time and thus have only limited interests in longer-term union benefits. However, such explanations are only partially satisfactory. The rise of households headed by females makes many women "breadwinners" in the traditional male sense, forcing a long-term labor force attachment. But few women work in sectors of traditional union strength, such as mining, contract construction, and transportation, meaning that women entering the labor force are not automatically covered by labor agreements. Another reason for organizing difficulties may lie in the fact that most union leaders and organizers are male. Even in such tradi-

---

[4]It should be noted that the fast-growing employee associations contain a high proportion of females. In 1974, over 55 percent (1.5 million) of all association members were female. As these associations are transformed into labor unions, female union membership will rise dramatically.

tionally female industries as garment manufacturing and textiles, males have dominated union leadership.

Although women have not yet been recognized as a group deserving a special department within the AFL-CIO, white-collar workers (including many women) have been recognized. White-collar employees present special organizing problems. Often better educated, they tend to accept and often adopt management attitudes, including promotion by merit rather than seniority and sometimes complex wage structures which reflect merit and effort rather than the uniformity characteristic in the blue-collar world. Many white-collar employees hope for promotions to management circles and consider unions as dangerous interferences in that quest. Finally, white-collar workers often work in disparate small groups or even in isolation, preventing the natural bond which links production workers.

Despite these obstacles, white-collar unions have made significant strides. As noted, white-collar unions in the public sector have been most successful; but unions organizing white-collar workers in the private sector have also enjoyed success, though limited in scope. The private sector has been more resistant to unionism, because private employers have more flexibility to assure advancement and often provide wage increases to white-collar workers when settlements with production workers are reached. In the public sector, increasing numbers have made white-collar workers aware that not everyone can be promoted, just as growing bureaucracy has increased the distance between top management and its white-collar staff. The result has been rapid white-collar union growth in the public sector, but only limited union gains in the private sector.

Some International Comparisons

The American labor movement is unique in several respects. Although it has one of the lowest *rates* of union organization (Table 3.2), the United States has more union members than any of its market-economy counterparts. In general, European labor movements usually have several competing confederations (associations of national unions such as the AFL-CIO) but fewer national unions than the United States.

Sweden and Belgium are the most organized market economies in the world (Table 3.2), with seven in ten workers organized into labor unions. Each labor movement is divided into several confederations, in Belgium along Socialist-Christian lines and in Sweden along occupational lines, the manual workers federation (LO) being the largest and strongest. In both countries, bargaining is typically centralized, resulting in industrywide or nationwide agreements, although local negotiations within the established national framework are permitted. These highly organized, centralized federations (employers are also organized into federations) have been very successful in minimizing strike activity in Sweden.

Table 3.2. Employment and Unionism:
Selected Countries, 1974

Country	Civilian Employment	Percent in Industry	Percent of Workers in Unions	Strike Activity*
Australia	5,736,000	35.1	52	n.a.
Belgium	3,801,000	41.0	70	184
Canada	9,137,000	31.1	28	1,156
France	21,096,000	39.2	20	208
Germany	25,689,000	47.6	37	49
Italy	18,715,000	44.1	20	1,723
Japan	52,010,000	37.0	34	270
Sweden	3,962,000	37.0	70	17
United Kingdom	24,767,000	42.3	44	664
United States	85,936,000	31.1	22	629

Sources: Employment and industrial distribution data from the Organization for Economic Cooperation and Development (Paris, 1977). Union data from *The Economist,* September 21, 1974. Strike data are from U.S. Department of Labor, *Handbook of Labor Statistics—1975* (Washington, D.C.: U.S. Government Printing Office, 1976).

*Days lost per thousand employees, 1974. Note that this measure varies considerably over time in individual countries.

Britain and Australia, with 44 and 52 percent organization, represent a different union model. Britain has nearly 500 separate unions (versus 175 in the United States), many of them extremely small craft unions. Although most of the largest unions are affiliated with the Trades Union Congress (TUC), the craft legacy has produced an almost universal respect for the picket line, allowing even the smallest craft unions formidable power as they strike and other unions honor their picket lines. In recent years, many British labor disputes produced plant shutdowns even though a union representing only 5 or 10 percent of the labor force was pressing a claim on the employer.

The Australian labor movement has its own peculiarities. Although Australia experienced economic growth, labor shortages, and immigration flows like those in the United States, Australian labor unions created and financed the Australian Labor Party. Defeats in the 1890s encouraged both political activity and caused the Australian labor movement to permit compulsory arbitration (mandatory submission of disputed issues to neutrals for decision), now a hallmark of Australian labor relations. In spite of arbitration, strikes are frequent, although of short duration. The 280 separate trade unions have 2.8 million members. The Australian Council of Trade Unions (ACTU), founded in 1927, contains about one half of all union members.

Both Britain and Australia have been subject to numerous strikes. But, while British and Australian strikes resemble their American counterparts— with picketing, strike benefits, and the expectation of sacrifice over time— strikes in Italy and France assume a different character. France has an organization rate of about 20 percent, lower than that in the United States, while Italian unions have organized from 20 to 40 percent of all workers, depending on how one measures the labor force. Both countries have a large, Communist-dominated union federation and several small competitors on the left and right. In France, for example, the Communist CGT, with 2.3 million members, is often outflanked on the left by the formerly Catholic CFDT with 900,000 members. A third federation, the FO, has 600,000 members, followed by federations of teachers, white-collar workers, and the remaining Catholics.

Unions in Italy and France collect very low dues—often less than $10 per member per year. This lack of income originally forced each federation to affiliate with a particular political party or religious organization for financial reasons, although the various union federations have attempted to maintain their independence in recent years. Strikes are common but are typically short, given the paucity of funds available to pay strike benefits. The shop-floor weakness of the unions in France and Italy (their lack of workplace representatives) often forces the unions to call "political strikes," general strikes directed as much at government actions (or inactions) as against employers.

The German Union Federation (DGB) is in part a creation of the postwar occupation authorities. To discourage the internecine strife which had characterized Weimar-era unions, the sixteen-union DGB was organized in 1949. One of the sixteen unions, IG Metall, is the world's largest "national," with 2.4 million members, nearly 25 percent of Germany's unionized work force. About 35 percent of Germany's 24 million workers are organized, but strikes are rare. Strike votes are mandatory, and strikes are permitted only if 75 percent of those voting in a secret ballot approve. The unions are financially secure, charging dues equivalent to about one percent of income.

German unions possess a unique voice in management decisions. Under the 1976 *Mitbestimmung* or codetermination law, each company's supervisory (Aufsichtsrat) board with 2,000 or more workers must contain equal numbers of labor and stockholder representatives. The result is a form of direct worker participation in management, especially in the longer-range planning for which the board of directors is responsible. A dispute over the proper role of senior management in codetermination (are they workers or management?) has thus far prevented the extension of "parity" workers' participation to smaller companies, but the German model has been adopted by Sweden and seriously considered in Holland and Britain.

In most European countries (except Britain), unions are supplemented by plant-level workers' councils. These councils, elected by all the plant's workers (not just union members), serve as the workplace handler of grievances and, increasingly, as the local bargaining agent for workers. Although some friction arises between the workers' council and unions, the fact that workers' council members are often union activists tends to minimize competition between the organizations.

The Japanese labor movement provides a final international comparison. Although unions with rights to organize, bargain, and strike were introduced only after World War II, some 12 million persons currently belong to Japan's 61,000 unions. This union proliferation results from the tendency for each plant or enterprise to have its own union. Most of these enterprise unions are, in turn, affiliated with federations along broadly defined craft lines, such as the Iron and Steelworkers Federation. The craft federations are organized into four national labor organizations which differ in their political orientation and labor militancy. Although some pressures to consolidate the labor movement have been felt, coordination is usually limited to the time of the annual "spring offensive," when unions traditionally press for annual wage gains. Lifetime employment security and seniority-based pay systems foster company loyalty, making strikes rare.

This brief sketch of foreign labor movements highlights both American uniqueness and international trends toward uniformity in labor relations. The American labor movement has long been regarded as the bastion of decentralized, localized bargaining, but pressures for more inclusive bargaining units in America and the rising importance of both local union organizations and plant-level works councils abroad point toward convergence in the relationship between centralized and localized bargaining. Despite an American tradition of avoiding dual or multiple unionism, in which several unions attempt to organize the same workers, the American labor force is among the least organized in the world. American unions typically adopt economically oriented, workplace bargaining stances, rather than attempting to enlist the political support for bargaining positions often sought elsewhere.

Summary

Unions are traditionally associated with blue-collar craft and industrial workers. As the economy undergoes its structural transformation, shifting from the production of goods to the provision of services, unions must shift the locus of their organizing efforts or see their share of those in the labor force decline. American unions have been slow to organize workers in the expanding service sector, and a growing labor force has reduced the union share of the labor force from 23.6 percent of all workers in 1960 to 20 percent in 1976.

The decreasing union share of the labor force is largely a result of the direction of economic (and hence employment) growth. But unions and associations in the expanding public, nonprofit (e.g. hospitals), and some private sectors have pursued vigorous organizing campaigns, doubling and tripling membership during the decade from 1966 to 1976. Future union growth will result from continued organizing drives among public employees and both white-collar and low-wage workers in the private sector.

In America, the 20 percent union share of the labor force is among the lowest in the market economies with whom the United States trades. Sweden and Belgium are the most organized countries in the world, with more than 70 percent of their labor forces enrolled in labor unions. In most countries, several confederations of unions (rather than only the AFL-CIO) coexist. These confederations or their constituent national unions often engage in centralized (e.g., nationwide) bargaining with employer groups. Although a convergence trend can be discerned, the American labor movement remains unique in its emphasis on decentralized bargaining (e.g., at each plant) and exclusive jurisdiction, with only one union to represent a group of workers.

Bibliography

Cain, Glen. *The Labor Force*. Madison, Wis.: Institute for Research on Poverty, 1974.

An excellent introduction to the concepts and measures used in defining the labor force and assessing trends.

Kassalow, Everett. *Trade Unions and Industrial Relations: An International Comparison*. New York: Random House, 1969.

An outstanding comparative analysis of the origin, structure, and functioning of the European and American labor movements.

U.S. Department of Labor, Bureau of Labor Statistics. *Directory of National and International Labor Unions*.

Issued biennially, the most recent issue is dated 1977 and contains 1974 data on trade unions and union membership. Supplements are issued periodically.

U.S. Department of Labor and U.S. Department of Health, Education, and Welfare. *Employment and Training Report of the President*. Washington, D.C.: U.S. Government Printing Office, 1977.

Contains an annual survey of labor force developments and research reports on various industries and subgroups as well as manpower policy information. The appendices provide a comprehensive set of current labor force data.

Trade Unions in Industrial Society

A trade union can be defined as an association of workers whose purpose is to improve *member* workers' *economic welfare* and *dignity,* primarily via *collective bargaining* with an employer. This definition is somewhat restrictive; the focus on collective bargaining as the primary instrument for seeking gains highlights characteristics of American unions and serves to exclude so-called near unions, the professional associations which perform some union functions. Under this definition, we immediately recognize such established industrial unions as the auto workers and steelworkers as well as the craft unions of, for example, carpenters and plumbers. Associations that perform union functions for members under different labels are often overlooked; the National Education Association, for one, utilizes both bargaining and political tactics in efforts to increase teacher salaries and benefits.[1] Although these associations are assuming an increasing importance, representing nearly one in seven organized workers, our theoretical survey will focus concern on more traditional trade unions.

Three types of labor organizations exist. The **craft unions,** which organize workers by skill (craft), are the oldest, dating from the advent of market competition and the Industrial Revolution. **Industrial,** or mass, **unions,** in which all workers in a particular plant or industry belong to a single union (regardless of skill), are more recent, awaiting both large-scale factory production and legislation that legalized and regularized organization procedures. The unionlike stance of **professional associations** is most recent. Originally established as societies to interchange ideas, to enforce "professional standards," and to lobby for favorable legislation or respectable public images, the competition of growing numbers and bureaucracy has frequently spurred the transformation of these formerly quiescent associations into militant labor unions. Although all three types of organizations currently exist, the theories of unionism's origins center largely on the emergence of craft unions.

---

[1]Other associations perform unionlike functions by enforcing licensing or quality standards. The American Medical Association, for example, helps exert upward pressures on doctor incomes by restricting the number of new doctors who can be trained and by enforcing minimum fee schedules for practicing physicians.

Why Workers Join Unions

If trade unions arose with industrialism, that is, production of goods (rather than agricultural commodities) in organizations (factories) with the assistance of capital (machinery), what are the features of industrialism that generate the trade union response among the work force? The traditional theories of unionism's origins revolve around the disruptive impact of capitalist entrepreneurs on existing production and marketing relations. In addition to inducing disruptive change, new production and marketing arrangements engender a class or group consciousness among those affected, providing a basis for joint action. The result is a "new class," workers who are free to offer their services in the labor market but who are dependent on employers for income, security, and status.

In a more modern context, the fact that industrialism can occur under a variety of political and economic systems (capitalism, socialism, fascism, nationalism, and so on) implies that the impingement of *some* disruptive force, be it capitalist or nationalist, induces protest. Into a relatively static, usually agrarian society is thrust a disruptive industrialism, upsetting existing institutions and the patterns of life, work, and status associated with them. As with any societal change, some segments of the populace will be hurt, some helped, and some unaffected. In most instances, industrialism threatens the labor aristocracy under the old institutions—artisans or craftsmen whose products can now be produced by cheaper labor with machinery. The expansion of internal and external markets increases competition while the division of labor associated with factory production undermines the position of established craftsmen. Historically, as we saw in Chapter 2, the threatened craftsmen formed defensive "trade" unions to preserve common prices in trade for their products.

If the threatening of a privileged position induces organization among craftsmen, what forces generate organization among the mass of industrial workers? Industrialization and factory work generate different modes of production relationships. They change the *dependency* relationship by making the worker rely on an impersonal business organization for both (1) a job and (2) a living wage associated with the job. These new production arrangements also effect a new *authority* relationship in the workplace, giving the employer control over the security of the worker's job tenure. Organization, by presenting a credible threat to the employer, tends to *equalize* the economic relationship and *rationalize* the employment relationship; that is, the union acts to guarantee job security and income while negotiating rules and procedures which preclude arbitrary employer actions against individual workers. Collective rather than individual bargaining increases the bargaining strength of the individual worker.

Threats to an established position, arbitrary employer actions, and the need for increased bargaining strength are the primary factors encouraging voluntary unionism. It must be recognized, however, that many people employed by large industrial firms are covered by **union shop** agreements, allowing individuals little choice (except in representative elections) in union membership decisions. Under a union shop clause, employers may hire anyone, but within a specified period (not less than thirty days), the new employee must join the union (and maintain his or her membership) or face discharge. (**Agency shop** agreements require all employees to pay union dues but do not require union membership. In an **open shop,** an employee is not required to join the union or pay dues.) Craft unions can sometimes maintain effective **closed shops** by operating **hiring halls,** under which anyone referred for work must already be a member of the union (or join the established union within seven days). Today, union shop agreements and closed shop arrangements account for a significant proportion of new union members.

The Labor Problem

The new dependency and authority relationships wrought by industrialization are the basis of employee-employer conflict, the "labor problem." The conflict arises because of change, change over which the dependent worker has little or no control. Economic theory has ignored the labor problem because it assumes that changes are costless and instantaneous. Under an (assumed) harmonious capitalism, this easy labor mobility makes protective trade unions redundant; any individual unhappy with his or her current job's rewards merely moves to another job, given the assumption of costless mobility and full employment.[2] Thus, economic theory views the exchange of labor time for wages like any other voluntary transaction. Since unions impede mobility and production flexibility by erecting rules, they restrict the flow of resources, slowing the speed with which economic change occurs.

The economist's view retains adherents. It has limited impact in economic policy making, however, because of several fallacious assumptions. No society has ever maintained full employment, meaning that job changes are rarely instantaneous and "free."[3] A variety of institutions, in both unionized and nonunion firms, serve to limit mobility by providing more benefits with increased service. **Seniority,** protecting the individual from layoffs and giving

---

[2]Economists have examined the nature of job search and the costs of unemployment. The idea that labor adjustments are required in any dynamic economy has received increased attention in the 1960s and 1970s, primarily because of the recognition that government often initiates labor adjustment processes. Awareness of the governmental role in causing labor displacement is found in the Trade Adjustment Assistance Act (1974), the Regional Rail Reorganization Act (1975), and the Redwoods National Park Expansion Act (1978).

[3]The United States and Western Europe have made great strides in cushioning the economic impacts of change. Unemployment insurance limits losses from layoffs, workmen's compensation assures income in the event of workplace injury, and welfare payments are sometimes available to those with little income and few assets. Indeed, some argue that the expansion of social welfare programs has fundamentally altered the "fear factor" which once made workers scarcity conscious and security prone. The demise of the traditional "scarcity psychology" is sometimes adduced as a factor promoting strikes, especially in the public sector.

him preference in intraplant job changes, as well as pension, health, and other fringe benefits, are all tied to length of service. If an experienced worker is dissatisfied in his own company, he must weigh his dissatisfaction against the losses incurred from beginning at the bottom in another company.

The costs of job changes are one reason a dissatisfied worker may elect to stay and fight rather than simply transferring employments. More important, workers form protective organizations because they fear arbitrary employer actions. The labor transaction is unlike other exchanges because the worker cannot be separated from his work. A simple exchange merely involves the surrender of one commodity (e.g., money) for another; the commodity itself has no voice in the matter. But a worker is unlike a ton of steel; after agreeing to work at a given wage, there is supervision to ensure that a proper degree of *effort* is expended. This ''effort bargain'' is renegotiated continually in the workplace, and without an established personnel policy or a trade union, the individual is subject to arbitrary discharge or unfavorable work assignments. Workplace equity, assured through informal work group rules, an established personnel procedure (in nonunion plants), or a trade union, remains the concern which distinguishes the labor input from others in the production process.

Trade unions fulfill other roles often overlooked in the analysis of their economic impacts. Since production processes are hierarchical, the worker is subordinate to various levels of management. Periodic negotiations put employer and labor representatives on an equal footing, perhaps fulfilling desires of employees for at least a limited period of power equality. In addition to the psychological benefits which may flow from union membership, worker organizations have a tradition of concern for the less fortunate in society. The labor movement is often the primary force behind protective labor legislation for both union and nonunion workers and the social welfare legislation which also benefits those not in the labor force.

Trade Unions in Industrial Society

The first unions emerged as local protective devices, aiming to slow or control the pace of disruptive change. As responses to the effects of actions initiated by others, unions are limited by the importance of the local disruptive agent, the local entrepreneur. As businesses and markets expand, so do trade unions, building on a series of local unions. National trade unions become constituent elements of a pluralistic society, exerting their influence to benefit members and, frequently, other groups with little or no political power.

Unions have purposes and goals at two distinct levels. At the local or company level, the union acts as the individual union member's representative in dealings with an employer. In the negotiation of a collective agreement and the administration of the resulting contract, the union is performing its *agency* function—that is, its role as collective agent or intermediary for a group of workers. This representative or agency role explains the origins of trade unions and remains unionism's *raison d'etre*.

Although unions exist as representative agencies, they are also vital components of the larger society, shaping and being shaped by socioeconomic changes. At a point in time, unions, management, and various interest groups seek to influence public policy in order to benefit their own constituencies. The relative success of separate interest groups is contingent on political power as well as the ability to form coalitions in support of particular policies. Unions may be allied with public interest groups to seek increases in the minimum wage or more public service jobs but join with business to oppose environmental legislation which may lessen product sales. These latter coalitions, often criticized, acknowledge the fact that the union is dependent on the employer for jobs; if the employer disappears, so do the jobs of union members.

Current union attitudes toward policy coalitions are largely dictated by rational calculation of the policy's impact on the union movement. It was not always so. Unions remained illegal associations until relatively recently. Even after workers were granted the right to organize and employers were obliged to bargain with employee representatives, unions won only grudging acceptance. Employers' hostility to the union quest for recognition, prompted in large part by the difficulty of getting an entrepreneur to surrender control over a production process often personally established, accounts for much of the violence that colors American labor history. If employers would not recognize the legitimacy of unions, how could unions acknowledge that capitalist entrepreneurs deserved a place in society? Until legitimacy and mutual toleration are established, class warfare is as likely as social stability.

Recognition and legitimacy were initial union goals. After achieving recognition, union behavior is shaped by the economic and social forces that influence the larger society. A variety of interdependent factors—economic, political, and social—influence the course of the modern economy and the actions of participants in it.

Some of the most important influences on labor relations in modern societies are the socioeconomic impacts of technological and organizational change. Modern technology both demands and makes possible specialization in production. Specialization is, in turn, accentuated by large-scale organization. Rather than having small entrepreneurs exercise personal command over production (and the work force involved), the modern industrial society is dominated by corporations, "juristic persons" designed to achieve efficiency. These corporate organizations, structured along hierarchic lines, often become depersonalizing bureaucracies. The result is a production system composed of complex bureaucracies in which the individual employee appears an insignificant element. The ensuing sense of individual powerlessness does much to explain the turn to representative organizations for workers.[4]

---

[4]As markets and corporations expand, so do their trade unions. The union itself begins to assume many of the depersonalizing attributes of the business organization, leading to cells within the union and (sometimes) defiance of union leaders—that is, both "big business" and "big labor" may be opposed by rank-and-file members.

The corporate organization, dominant in industrial society, is motivated by a set of goals. Whether these goals are profit, market share, or corporate size, the corporate bureaucracy typically attempts to achieve these goals with rational or efficiency-conscious management. Rational decision making requires a uniform measure or yardstick, leading to the use of money measures to stimulate and reward productive effort. Werner Sombart described business rationality as a planned search for efficiency dominated by "the 'cash nexus' [which] regulates all economic activity, [so] that everywhere and always a surplus is sought for."[5]

Although the rationality which permeates modern corporate bureaucracy often alienates the work force, it also facilitates unionism. The entrepreneur who begins and personally commands a business enterprise is loathe to surrender authority to unions, often viewing them as personal threats rather than simply another institution which must be dealt with. The modern corporation, dominated by professional management (Galbraith's technostructure), more readily accepts unions. In the absence of personal convictions, corporate rationality can more easily weigh the costs and advantages of unionism without ideological conviction.

Corporate rationality can be a successful organizing device only if the labor force is willing to respond to its rewards. Planning and decision making based on monetary measures is simplified if the labor force responds to monetary rewards; the manufacturer of a product must know, for example, if the labor force will work at the planned wage before deciding whether the project will be profitable. Since the cash basis of society is so recent (and still evolving in much of the world), corporate rationality is also of recent vintage.

Modern industrial society, dominated by corporate bureaucracies, shapes and is in turn shaped by government. We have already noted the growing importance of the state in industrial relations, but the impact of government goes much further. Government assumes responsibility for providing socioeconomic infrastructure; the laws and regulations governing money, weights, and measures; and for regulating and enforcing the contracts necessary to facilitate business transactions. The infrastructure role is traditional and universal; what is new in American society is the growth of state regulatory functions in civil rights, safety, and business ethics; the rising importance of government as a consumer of (especially military) goods; and the expansion of the state's social welfare function, an expansion meant to cushion the adjustments and dislocations of a dynamic, technological society.

The role of the state in the modern economy is a contentious issue. Both management and labor attempt to use the state for their own ends—management to reduce production uncertainties while maintaining profit-making flexibility and labor to strengthen its own bargaining position by erecting social

---

[5]Werner Sombart, *The Jews and Modern Capitalism* (New York: Collier Books, 1962), p. 162.

welfare minima which provide a bargaining floor. The ability of the competing interests to use the state for parochial ends has vacillated over time, the state being largely probusiness until the 1930s, prolabor between 1935 and 1948, and more neutral since then. The achievement and maintenance of an equilibrium between competing management and labor interests helps explain the relative economic and social stability in modern America. Other societies, swinging more rapidly from one pole to another, have often been less successful in the quest for economic prosperity.

Comparative Labor Movements

If industrialization and its disruptions are *the* cause of trade unionism, and if the labor problem is universal because of the peculiarities of labor in production, what accounts for the observed differences in the behavior of a labor movement over time? What factors explain why trade unions differ across societies at a single point in time? Every nation has at least an implicit system for resolving inevitable labor conflict, for promoting labor peace and minimizing the effects of labor disputes. These systems, dependent on socioeconomic, political, and historical circumstance, present a myriad of approaches to a common social problem.

The various systems for resolving labor conflict can be distinguished by the presence or absence of trade unions, the relationship between unions and government, and the structure and functioning of the unions themselves. In countries with unions, labor movements differ in terms of: (1) their relative use of economic and political instruments to achieve union goals; (2) the degree of labor movement identification with larger state goals; and (3) the structure of trade unionism and the coverage and content of collective bargaining. In America, trade unions rely primarily on economic bargaining to achieve union goals. Unions accept the larger social structure of market capitalism, seeking to reform rather than overthrow it. Finally, the American labor movement relies on its own leaders to negotiate contracts with employers in an atmosphere relatively free of public constraint.

European labor movements are often closely allied with a political party. Feudalism had made class differences explicit and, with its dissolution, (socialist) political parties arose to represent the "working class." In most European societies except Britain, the labor movement was founded and nurtured by a class-based political party, helping explain the class (us-them) attitude of contemporary European unions. Close political ties made political instruments far more attractive to European unions than in America; indeed, in Britain, the labor movement founded the Labour Party. The variety of political and religious movements spawned an array of union groupings, with federations of, for example, Catholic unions, socialist unions, and communist unions, competing with each other as well as with employers.

The centralization of political life helps account for the "top-down" structure of European unionism. The American federation of unions, the AFL-CIO, has no substantive impact on collective bargaining or day-to-day union activities. In Europe, national union (con)federations are usually far more important, often negotiating industrywide (rather than company-by-company) contracts, controlling strike funds, and lobbying for protective labor legislation. Because European bargaining is more centralized, national agreements can be made to conform to government economic policies, although national leaders have had increased difficulty in preventing local dissatisfaction with such "sacrifices" from generating **wildcat strikes.**

Although the hallmarks of American unionism—strong local unions, detailed company contracts, and exclusive jurisdiction (one union per plant or company)—are not pronounced in Europe, surrogates exist. The American local typically funnels worker ideas to negotiators and acts as the union representative in grievance settlement. In Europe, workers' councils at each plant perform a similar grievance function. Although frequently dominated by union members, these workers' councils act as independent local bodies for regulating working conditions and handling grievances in the absence of strong union locals and detailed collective agreements. In part, these workers' councils are logical because of the lack of exclusive jurisdiction in much of Europe. Rather than one union per plant, as in the United States, European plants typically contain locals from several competing unions. A workers' council provides a unifying influence at the local level by acting as the central local body, independent of competing unions.

European and American labor movements emerged under similar patterns of industrialization. In currently developing societies, differences in industrialization patterns affect the origin, structure, and behavior of the nascent trade unions. Unemployment and underemployment in agriculture are typically pandemic, causing "labor queues" for entry into the relatively higher-paying modern sector. An inability to check this flow of labor into the modern industrial sector, as well as the high degree of state intervention in the economy, forces the trade unions in developing countries to revert to political rather than economic strategies. But even political tactics are limited. Many trade union movements were deeply involved in liberation struggles. Although the unions were originally revolutionary in outlook, union ties to political leaders and the simple inability of governments in developing countries to provide benefits limit the gains which most unions can extract for members. Union movements in these countries typically subordinate their parochial goals to the overall goal of economic development, or break with the political leadership to extract benefits in those sectors where skill levels can limit the labor influx, such as transportation and communication.

In developing nations, unions often arise before the disruptive impacts of industrialization are widespread, when the industrial labor force is less than 5 percent of the total labor force. The unions that do emerge in such circumstances are often formed and led by nonworking intellectuals more interested in class-based struggle than in day-to-day bargaining and contract administration. These nonworking leaders, often involved with several unions simultaneously, have minimal appreciation for the workplace concerns that long dominated American unionism. Over time, however, the intellectual union founders have been replaced by former workers, lending one converging aspect to unionism which began under radically different socioeconomic circumstances.

The simple replacement of intellectuals with workers does not assure that unions in currently developing societies will evolve to resemble their American or European counterparts. The absence of a significant indigenous class of craftsmen denies the nascent unions "natural leaders" and a base from which to select them. The fact that industrialization often occurs with foreign capital, motivated to enter the country because of the ready availability of cheap labor, forces the unions to adopt an industrial stance and confront a sophisticated management from the outset. The resulting strategic importance of the industrialized labor force makes the loyalty of the unions a prime target of those in power and those competing for power. To retain control, the state often intercedes, granting wages and fringe benefits to selected groups of workers. The wooing of an already privileged segment of the labor force, although industrial rather than craft oriented, injects a political dimension into labor relations in developing countries which may override the attention to workplace concerns so characteristic of American unionism.

Labor Movement Theory

Theories of the labor movement attempt to discern the common patterns in union formation and development which explain both current union structure and function and predict future labor relations policies. The best-known theory is Marxism, which equated capitalism and industrialization and predicted that inevitable capitalist actions would be self-destructive. The capitalist system forced continued capital accumulation, an accumulation that decreased profit rates. Profit rates could be maintained only if capitalists succeeded in capturing foreign markets through imperialistic expansion and/or if the working class was subjected to increased exploitation. Ever-increasing exploitation, marked by longer hours, production speedups, and lower wages, eventually produced a situation in which the working class realized that it had "nothing to lose but its chains" and rose up to "expropriate the expropriators."

The Marxist theory is as much a theory of economic development as a theory of trade unionism. In Lenin's reformulation of Marxism, trade union consciousness arose spontaneously from workplace exploitation. Although a spontaneous and inevitable outcome of capitalist production methods, trade unions did not develop a life and purpose of their own unless socialist intellectuals assumed control and used the union as a device to imbue class consciousness and class protest. The class nature of unionism favored industrywide rather than craft organization, since industrial unions help overcome divisions along skill levels. Socialist (or communist) influence in the American labor movement was prominent (but not dominant) until the postwar era, when "infiltrators" were expelled from American unions.

The American school of labor movement theorists was dominated by two University of Wisconsin professors, John R. Commons and Selig Perlman. Like the Marxists, they identified capitalist production techniques as the source of worker discontent. Unions arose as protest organizations, designed to halt an increased worker exploitation which arose, not from capitalism as such, but from market expansion and competition. Journeymen or skilled craftsmen typically worked in small groups to produce shoes, hats, coats, and so on. Although one person was a "master" journeyman, wages were dictated by the price the master obtained for the product rather than the number of hours worked. This master-journeyman relationship led to a common interest—both wanted "reasonable" prices (hence wages) for their products.

Population growth and market expansion changed this friendly relationship. More customers increased both the number of production shops and the number of journeymen working for each master. Growing size replaced personal workplace relationships with impersonality. Soon masters did not enter the shop. Instead, they became merchant-capitalists who traveled to secure new markets for their products. As the output of each shop increased, so did specialization and uniformity. Because merchant-capitalists were in competition to sell goods, they began employing less-skilled apprentices to make *parts* of shoes, hats, and coats for an hourly wage rather than a wage based on the price of the final product.

The journeymen viewed the competition induced by market expansion and the division of labor as a threat to their privileged position. Rather than having the same interests as the merchant-capitalist (a high price for the product), journeymen became concerned about wages as the link between prices and wages was broken. The result—organizations of craftsmen to confront the merchant-capitalist in the workplace, the early craft unions. For Commons, the competitive price cutting induced by market expansion was the direct cause of organization among skilled laborers.

After the emergence of unions, what factors account for their behavior? Commons viewed the unions as one of the power blocs in a pluralistic society, existing to protect those economically and socially weak. Commons believed that friction between power groups could upset social equilibrium, that only the existence of countervailing power forces could preserve the stability necessary for economic progress. Commons's student, Selig Perlman, explored another facet of unionization. A Russian expatriate, Perlman sought to explain why the behavior of American trade unionism seemed "organic" or natural, to explain why the Marxist prediction that trade unions would be vanguard revolutionary forces was wrong in the American case.

In Perlman's view, society consists of optimistic, expansion-minded businessmen; pessimistic, scarcity-conscious workers, and intellectuals bent on destroying capitalism.[6] The capitalist class is the dynamic force in society, seeing new business opportunities, taking risks, and driving society forward. The disruptions imposed by capitalist innovation and drive dislocate the security-conscious manual worker. In a world with unemployed people, workers band together to exert job control, control over how to divide up the available work among the work group. The result is "organic unionism," not bent on destroying or replacing the employer, as Marx held, but merely on reforming or exerting some control over the employer's actions.

Left to their own devices, Perlman held, unions would become reform movements with only workplace concerns, not revolutionary social forces. But Perlman believed that organic unions are not allowed unfettered expression of their natural objectives. The working class can serve as a vehicle which permits intellectuals to assume power, making threats to the control of unions from outside intellectuals omnipresent. If these reformist or revolutionary intellectuals achieve power, the union is diverted from its true workplace functions to expend its energies in politics, an arena which Perlman held to be of limited use to organic unionism.

In Perlman's theory, the behavior of a labor movement at any point in time reflects the interplay of the three contending psychologies. In his comparative analysis, Perlman found the "will to power" of the Russian capitalists weak because they refused any compromises that may have forestalled revolution. The Russian unions were not allowed to develop along their natural path because of intellectual domination, permitting the Russian Revolution of 1917. In the United States, by contrast, the capitalist class was both entrenched and flexible. Private property rights were respected because of the mass of farmers and small businessmen, class distinctions were blurred because of the absence of feudalism and the constant influx of immigrants who believed in upward mobility, and revolutionary intellectuals were unable to secure a foothold in the labor unions. The result was a dynamic capitalism and a labor movement that evolved, in Perlman's terms, along its natural or inevitable course.

Both Marxist and the Commons-Perlman labor movement theories have been modified and extended by students of the labor movement. No single theory dominates. In part, this difficulty arises from the nature of labor theorizing—how does one generalize about a movement whose manifestations are the result of both universal and specific trends? The miscellany of union movements and features testifies to the importance of local influences, local influences whose presence may make the general theory of secondary import.

The most comprehensive "modern" theoretical survey of industrial rela-

---

[6]"In an economic community, there is a separation between those who prefer a secure, though modest return . . . and those who play for big stakes and are willing to assume risk in proportion. The first compose the great bulk of manual workers of every description . . . while the latter are, of course, the entrepreneurs and the big businessmen." In contrast, "the intellectual [tends] to think of labor as an abstract 'mass' in the grip of an abstract 'force' . . . that labor is somehow the 'chosen vessel' of whatever may be the power which shapes the destiny of society." (*The Theory of the Labor Movement,* pp. 238–239, 280–281.)

tions systems was provided by John Dunlop in 1958. In Dunlop's formulation, an industrial relations system is comprised of actors, contexts, a binding ideology, and a body of rules to govern the interrelationship of system participants. Each of the separate system influences—actors, contexts, ideology, and rules—is subject to change with economic evolution, permitting the entire industrial relations system to be transformed with socioeconomic development.

Dunlop's "actors" are management, workers, and government (representatives). Both workers and management are organized into hierarchies which interact, as when management issues orders to work and workers respond. Governmental actors assume multiple roles, sometimes acting as employers but usually serving to define the framework for private interaction.

Industrial relations actors operate in an environment shaped by technology, market constraints, and the distribution of power in society at large. Technology plays a vital role in shaping labor-management interaction. It defines the size, location, and pace of work as well as influencing the size of the work group, the context of jobs, and the hours of work. Just as technology affects industrial relations by influencing the organization and nature of work, the nature of the product market shapes the size of the management enterprise, the degree of product market competition, and the characteristics of the labor force. National markets, for example, are associated with large-scale enterprise, often operating in oligopolistic markets with relatively skilled and stable labor forces.

In Dunlop's theory, both technology and market conditions are shaped by the distribution of power in society at large. In some instances, power relationships in the industrial relations system may mirror power relations in the larger society, but they need not do so. Unions may be relatively weak in dealings with employers but stronger in society at large, as suggested in France. Some unions are strong at local (plant) levels but relatively weak on broader, societywide levels. The distribution of power helps structure the overall system of labor relations as well as influencing particular labor-management interactions.

The industrial relations system is held together by an ideology, which reflects itself in work-related rules. A network or web of rules is established to mediate inevitable conflicts peacefully—defining, for example, the roles of management, unions, and government in specific disputes. The establishment of rules channels conflict into well-defined forums for discussion and resolution, avoiding the necessity to resort to frequent power conflicts in the workplace. The rule-making process reflects the system's binding ideology, a belief in peaceful dispute settlement rather than continuous, class-generated clashes. Since different societies exhibit wide variation in actors, contexts, ideologies, and rules, industrial relations systems appear in a variety of designs and purposes.

Despite the variation across trade unions, labor movements do seem to share several common creeds. Sidney and Beatrice Webb, British labor historians at the turn of the century, identified the Device of the Common Rule and the Device of the Restriction of Numbers as two philosophies permeating all unions. The Common Rule doctrine, which they embraced, makes individual bargaining unnecessary; all workers are employed under a standard wage structure and similar working conditions, preventing employers from showing preferences or victimizing individual workers. The Restriction Rule, decried as parochial by the Webbs, is more important (at local levels) in craft unions. If the number of jobs is limited, the union can maintain its bargaining power by limiting entry to the craft with, for example, apprenticeship regulations. Industrial union demands for full employment perform a similar function; if unemployment is reduced, bargaining power can be increased.

Summary

Workers join trade unions to protest the disruptions associated with change. This change is an inevitable concomitant of industrialization and mass production. Although it was once felt that industrialization and capitalism were equivalent, it is now clear that there are many roads to industrialization. Whatever the rubric, the labor problem, arising from inevitable conflicts of interest in employment, is universal. In the modern industrial society, technology, bureaucracy, rationality, and state intervention together shape labor relations.

American labor relations differ in several respects from those in other industrialized nations and in currently developing nations. The American labor movement is unique in the strong emphasis it places on ecomomic bargaining instead of political action, its importance at the local or plant level, and its mild reformist stance. The American school of labor theorists saw this nonrevolutionary union attitude as the natural maturing of an organic union movement, one allowed to develop without outside interference.

Bibliography

Dunlop, John. *Industrial Relations Systems.* New York: Holt, Rinehart and Winston, 1958.

The first comprehensive statement of the idea that labor relations result from interacting participants within a definable system.

Kerr, Clark, et al. *Industrialism and Industrial Man: The Problems of Labor and Management in Economic Growth.* Cambridge, Mass.: Harvard University Press, 1960.

An ambitious attempt to identify the type of labor relations system which evolves in terms of the type of change-inducing elite and the disruptions it provokes.

Perlman, Mark. *Labor Union Theories in America: Background and Development.* Evanston, Ill.: Row and Peterson, 1958. Reprinted 1976.

The best survey of the older theories of the labor movement.

Perlman, Selig. *A Theory of the Labor Movement.* New York: Kelly, 1928.

The classic explanation of why the American labor movement is the model of business or job-conscious unionism.

Union Structure and Government

5

Unions evolved as local combinations of workers with no innate organizational structure or government. As unions (and businesses) expanded, organizational complexity increased. Since collective bargaining is a relationship between organizations, analyzing union structure and its impacts on the bargaining process enables us to understand the central purpose of labor unions. Unions are governed by a range of leadership styles, running the gamut from democracy to dictatorship. Democracy in union government is favored on both humanitarian grounds and because an avowed purpose of unionism is to introduce democracy into the workplace.

Since unions are reactive bodies, dependent on employers to create the jobs over which the union exercises control, union structure is responsive to the structure of the industry or industries in which it organizes. Unions combine shop floor organizations into locals, which, in turn, are organized into a national union (or international, given Canadian members). Most national unions are affiliated with the American Federation of Labor-Congress of Industrial Organizations (AFL-CIO). It is at the local or intermediate level that the union dependence on industry structure is apparent. In industrial unions, locals and intermediate regional offices are concentrated where employment (and membership) is concentrated; for example, the United Auto Workers Union (UAW) is concentrated in Michigan, and the United Steelworkers Union (USW) is most prominent in western Pennsylvania and eastern Ohio.

The trade union is a political organization. Both local and national officers are usually elected at periodic conventions for defined terms of office. Tenure at the top is typically lifelong after election, but leadership turnover at the local level is quite common. The political nature of the union makes its intraorganizational behavior resemble a legislative body more closely than its business adversary, but the extent to which unions should reflect membership diversity remains unresolved. Business organizations have hierarchical structures with well-developed lines of authority, permitting decisions to be made quickly. Democracy is the time-consuming process of achieving compromise—to the extent that unions actually permit authority to flow from bottom to top, union decision-making processes are slowed.

Under national labor law, a union selected to represent a group of workers has the **exclusive bargaining rights** for those workers on all matters concerning "wages, hours, and other conditions of employment." The employer cannot, for example, decide to give some employees a wage increase without first conferring with the union. Such a delegated responsibility gives the union enormous power, and this power has prompted government regulation of the relationship between the union and its members to ensure that the union represents its members fairly. The Railway Labor Act (1926) is explicit on this duty of union "fairness" to its membership: "The organization chosen to represent a craft is to represent all its members, the minority as well as the majority, and is to act for and not against those it represents." The difficulty of *always* acting fairly toward all members in situations which demand internal unity has made union democracy among the most debated issues in labor relations.

This chapter reviews the structure of American unionism, its sources of revenue, and internal union procedures. Although instances of union corruption and antidemocratic behavior do recur, it may be prudent to remember that unions are among that rare set of institutions in society whose leaders are drawn from workers in each plant, workers initially selected and hired by the union's bargaining adversary, the employer.

Union Structure

Since the earliest unions were local groups of craftsmen, organization by craft or skill seemed an appropriate organizing dimension at the time that unionism emerged. Over time, the structure of the economy changed. Large-scale industry, in which the worker had an interest in both a particular skill as well as the fate of a particular company, created tensions between the AFL, which favored the craft basis of organization, and the CIO, which feared that splintering workers along craft lines would weaken internal unity. This dispute over the proper mode of organization was largely responsible for the formation of an independent CIO in 1935.

Today the dispute between the advocates of craft versus industrial organization is a moot issue. Some unions, notably the Teamsters, have evolved into "general unions," willing to organize groups of workers in any industry or occupation. Jurisdictional disputes between unions,[1] once common, are now less frequent.[2] When jurisdictional disputes between AFL-CIO unions arise, the

---

[1] A good example of such a jurisdictional dispute was the competition between the Teamsters (independent) and the United Farm Workers (AFL-CIO) to represent fieldworkers in California agriculture. The dispute raged for nearly a decade, despite intervention by both AFL-CIO leadership and Teamster officials. In 1977, after state law regularized the representative election process, the Teamsters withdrew, granting fieldworker jurisdiction to the UFW.

[2] If both unions are affiliated with the AFL-CIO, jurisdictional disputes are settled with established procedures under the Internal Disputes Plan. Between 1962 and 1975, an annual average of 125 disputes were appealed to the mediation panel of the AFL-CIO. Over half (56 percent) were

AFL-CIO has its own Internal Disputes Plan to encourage the parties to reconcile differences. In the event the AFL-CIO fails to settle the dispute, or if (one of) the unions are outside the AFL-CIO, the National Labor Relations Board (NLRB) can certify *any* union which wins a representation election as the bargaining representative of a particular group of workers.

National unions are built on **locals.** Each local comprises the union members of a department or departments, a single plant, a group of plants (amalgamated locals), or, in the craft unions, the workers in a given area. The 71,000 locals serve as the building blocks of the 177 national (or international) unions.[3] Most nationals are, in turn, affiliated with the AFL-CIO, the dominant American federation of national unions. The national union is the key element in union structure (Figure 5.1), since it is usually responsible for organizing new workers, negotiating or assisting in the negotiation of collective agreements, and maintaining internal union discipline. Unions affiliated with the AFL-CIO benefit from its assistance in organizing and bargaining and are subject to AFL-CIO strictures on internal discipline and financial conduct.

Each national union has a written constitution which details the duties and obligations of union officials, the constituent locals, and union members. The national union is governed by periodic conventions, usually annual or biennial. These conventions serve as a forum for local delegates to adopt resolutions, amend the constitution, and elect national union officers—usually a president, secretary, and several vice presidents. Between conventions, power rests with an elected executive board, a board often dominated by the union president. Incumbent officers have a great many advantages over potential rivals, including control of the union newspaper, exposure and name recognition among members, and influence over the conduct of the convention itself. Since most unions use the conventions for election purposes and because national union elections are frequently uncontested,[4] tenure in office is typically ten to twenty years. The effects of such tenure patterns are still debated; they can promote union stability but can also foster a dictatorial leadership.

The local is a creation of the national. When it accepts a charter from the national union, the local agrees to cede certain powers to the national, often

---

settled by mediation, 41 percent were decided by an impartial umpire, and 3 percent were pending. The AFL-CIO Executive Council can impose sanctions on unions failing to comply with an umpire's decision, but such sanctions were applied in only twenty instances. For elaboration, see the *Directory of National Unions and Employee Associations* (Washington, D.C.: U.S. Department of Labor, 1977), pp. 3–4.

[3]The thirty-five closely related national associations are composed of 14,000 local chapters, with each chapter representing, for example, the employees in a particular local government agency.

[4]One national union, the International Typographical Union (ITU), has institutionalized intra-union opposition. The 111,000 ITU members, who set type for the nation's newspapers, have long been considered part of the labor elite. Since the turn of the century, a two-part system has been maintained within the union. For an exhaustive analysis of the ITU, see S. Lipset, M. Trow, and J. Coleman, *Union Democracy: The Internal Politics of the International Typographical Union* (Glencoe, Ill.: The Free Press, 1956).

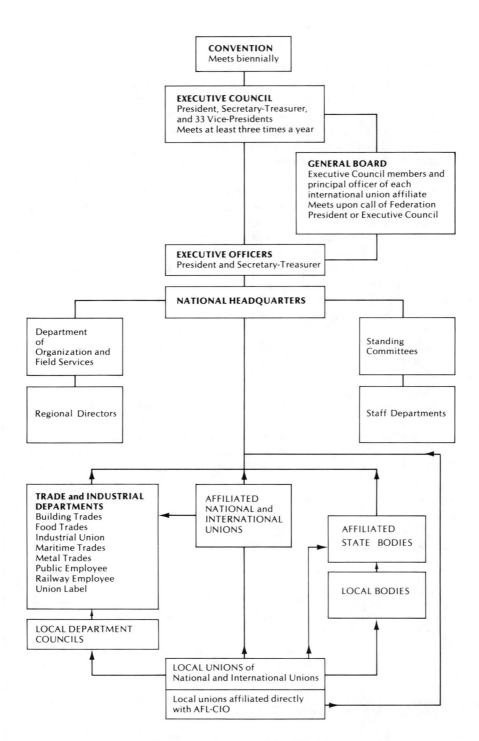

Figure 5.1. Structure of the AFL-CIO

including the role of final arbiter in agreement ratification, strike decisions, and member discipline. These locals, ranging from as few as 5 to as many as 40,000 members, are charged with organizing new workers, assisting members in both union and nonunion affairs, and negotiating (or providing assistance when negotiating) collective agreements. Because the local is a creation of the national, its charter can be revoked by national officers and the local placed in trusteeship (or receivership), that is, under the direct control of national union leaders.

The union local holds weekly or monthly membership meetings. As the union body closest to the workplace, the local is that part of the union with which the typical member is in most frequent contact. Local unions usually elect officials which parallel those on the national level—a president and a secretary-treasurer. In industrial unions, these posts are often unpaid, a factor which sometimes makes it difficult to secure candidates. Craft unions have elected officials as well as an elected or appointed business agent. Because craftsmen typically work for only short periods with any given employer, the business agent, the key official in local craft unions, is empowered to make immediate decisions on the merits of an individual grievance or the legality of a certain work procedure. It is this power to affect work immediately which sometimes permits local business agents to extract payments for *not* ordering a work shutdown or slowdown, a power which sometimes results in local union leaders enriching themselves at members' expense.

In addition to elected local officers, virtually all local unions have representatives in each plant or worksite included in the local. These (usually elected) representatives are the **shop stewards** (or grievance committeemen and, sometimes, plant representative). If the plant has several departments or works different shifts, there will usually be a union representative in each department and for every shift. It is the interaction between these union officials and their counterpart supervisors which is at the heart of day-to-day union-management relations; when, for example, workplace grievances arise, the initial attempt at resolution occurs between supervisor and shop steward. The relationship between supervisors and shop stewards largely determines the daily labor relations climate.

Local union leadership is sometimes criticized for being inefficient, undemocratic, or both. Local leaders often have little or no training, and leadership turnover is common. Member apathy is often widespread, prompting local unions to offer door prizes to induce attendance at local meetings. Recognizing the problem, the AFL-CIO and some public institutions offer courses in administration and negotiation for local union officials through labor colleges and workers' schools.

Local unions are often organized into intermediary or regional bodies. At this intermediary level, union dependence on industry structure is apparent. Union concentration follows employer concentration, with industrial unions typically combining the local unions from different plants of the same company—for example, the General Motors Bargaining Council of the United

Automobile Workers. Some local unions organize into joint boards (Teamsters) to coordinate bargaining demands, while others are coordinated in districts, as the United Mine Workers (UMW). In the building trades, local unions typically affiliate on a geographic basis, carrying out centralized bargaining with small and diverse contractors. In some instances, these intermediary bodies serve as a buffer between the national and its locals, further removing the national from its locals but sometimes providing a base for aspiring national union leaders to mount a challenge to incumbents.

In addition to regional and company associations, local unions organize into city and statewide federations to press for political gains. These city and state associations vary in importance. Among craft unions, local ''labor councils'' certify strikes, lending moral support and encouraging members of other unions to honor established picket lines. City centrals were the first organizations of local unions, antedating national unions by some thirty years. At the state level, the local union federation often exerts political pressures on labor's behalf, including, for example, lobbying activity to repeal state right-to-work laws and/or promoting particular candidates in political election.

National unions also combine into federations, forming the dominant American federation, the AFL-CIO. The AFL-CIO includes only 111 of the 177 national unions, but contains nearly 80 percent of all union members. Created by a merger between the previously separate AFL and CIO federations, the AFL-CIO has been led by George Meany since its inception in 1955. The two largest national unions, the Teamsters and the UAW, are not members of the AFL-CIO.

The AFL-CIO, like many of its national union constituents, is governed by a biennial convention. Between conventions, an Executive Council—composed of a president, secretary-treasurer, and thirty-three vice presidents (the leaders of various national unions)—governs the AFL-CIO. The General Board includes all members of the Executive Council and one officer from each AFL-CIO national union, with voting power determined by the number of dues-paying members each union has. Within the AFL-CIO, the national unions are autonomous. The AFL-CIO has no voice in collective bargaining and cannot even force national unions to adopt its political stances.[5] AFL-CIO power is limited because it possesses only one sanction against an offending union, expulsion from the federation. Given the limited compunction induced by expulsion (e.g., Teamster membership gains actually accelerated after expulsion), the AFL-CIO tends to exert only an indirect influence over its member unions.

The AFL-CIO's executive officers and committees meet periodically to adopt positions on issues affecting labor and social policy. But the AFL-CIO is organized to coordinate union activity on a variety of fronts. The eight trade and industrial departments group national unions by their fields of special interest, including groupings of national unions in the building trades, maritime

---

[5]Since the executive board includes national union leaders, AFL-CIO positions do not usually deviate from mainstream political feelings. However, the AFL-CIO usually endorses Democratic candidates, despite a tradition in certain building-trade unions to support Republicans.

trades, and railroads as well as the recently formed public employees department. The AFL-CIO has a Department of Organization and Field Services, which issues charters to organizing committees in jurisdictions not included in any member union's ambit and assists the various national unions in their own organizing efforts. In all these activities, the AFL-CIO usually serves as a facilitator, a mediator, or a forum for promoting joint action between several unions.

As noted, union structure is contingent on the structure of the industry in which it organizes. As industrial concentration increases, the number of separate national unions decreases (from 191 in 1966 to 177 in 1976). When a single company expands into several industries, assuming a "conglomerate" character, the union must either follow or be forced to deal with both other unions and the company. Some unions (e.g., those bargaining with General Electric) have attempted "coalition bargaining," in which several unions jointly bargain with a single company, but it is more common for the union to "follow the company" by expanding its jurisdiction from, for example, auto workers to agricultural implement and aerospace workers. As technological change eliminates the need for certain skills, such as blacksmithing, some unions disappear. In America, increasing industrial concentration has augmented the tendency toward more inclusive "general" unions such as the Teamsters, not tied to a particular industry or craft, but these general unions are still more common in Europe than in the United States. Pressures for union mergers continue, especially in such areas as the building trades, but unions have an innate reluctance to surrender autonomy by becoming part of a larger group.

Union power rests with those officials responsible for collective bargaining. If the national union negotiates contracts, power is vested in the president of the national. If bargaining is regional, as in trucking, power rests with regional officers. When bargaining is conducted at local levels, as in the building trades, union power is concentrated among local leaders. The structure of the industry is the most important single determinant of bargaining structure, illustrating union dependence on employers once again.[6]

The largest national unions have become major repositories of finance. In 1974, unions had an annual income of about $3.5 billion, assets of another $3.5 billion, and varying degrees of influence over the $145 billion assets of private pension funds. Union income is derived from dues (averaging about two hours' earnings per month), initiation fees, special assessments, and a return on investments. Local unions collect dues and fees, retaining about one half of all income received and passing the rest on to the national.

Unions are among that rare set of institutions which promote leaders, often

---

[6]A few union leaders have been able to structure bargaining and union power to suit their own ends. While president of the Teamsters Union, James Hoffa was able to transfer previously regional power to the national office. With Hoffa's demise, power once again reverted to regional offices. For an outstanding analysis of Hoffa's acquisition and use of power, see Ralph and Estelle James, *Hoffa and the Teamsters: A Study of Union Power* (Princeton: D. Van Nostrand, 1965).

selected by a bargaining adversary (the employer), "up from the ranks."
Employees are selected for their on-the-job abilities, not their administrative or
organizational talents. Employees who do demonstrate managerial skills are
often promoted within *management,* not the union. Given the discretionary
powers of certain local union officers, notably the business agent in the building
trades, it is perhaps more surprising that instances of financial malfeasance and
corruption are rare rather than commonplace.

The union corruption which does occur assumes a variety of forms. Some
(primarily local) union leaders enrich themselves by obtaining bribes for signing **sweetheart contracts**—agreements favorable to the employer. Leaders can
benefit without employer cooperation by selling supplies to the union at inflated
prices, borrowing money from the union at favorable terms, or simply embez-
zling funds. Union leaders can extort payments from employers for failing to
call a strike or for overlooking certain provisions of the collective bargaining
agreement. In the past, such union leader actions were more common, especially in the building trades and among teamsters. Sometimes outside racketeers
can assume control of local unions. When the Capone organization infiltrated
local unions in Chicago during the 1930s, it is estimated that a majority of
Chicago businessmen were forced to make some type of payoff to ensure labor
peace.

Union Leaders and Union Members

Although corruption and racketeering among unions seem to have decreased, the proper relationship between union leadership and membership remains ambiguous. Union pressures for the closed shop (where one must be a
union member *before* securing employment) were often opposed because the
closed shop effectively delegated the legal power to allocate certain jobs to a
private group, the union leadership, a delegation of authority which Congress
was not entitled to make. But if unions are denied permission wholly to regulate entry to a job, they can still govern exit from particular jobs with internal
disciplinary procedures. This union power to affect an individual's livelihood,
especially after seniority and skills have been acquired, accounts for the legal
tendency to view unions more as public utilities than private associations.

Until 1959, government intervention in internal union affairs was minimal.
Labor unions were viewed as private associations, free to adopt their own codes
of internal conduct. Court intervention was limited to union handling of funds,
since money involved property and the courts had ample precedent for regulating the use of property. The growing economic power of unions, the realization
that unions often influence the livelihood of members, and exposure of malfeasance and corruption within the Teamsters Union in the late 1950s led to calls
for more direct government regulation of internal union affairs. After two years
of testimony before the McClellan Committee, the Labor-Management Reporting and Disclosure Act (LMRDA) of 1959 was enacted. The LMRDA, usually

called the Landrum-Griffin Act, permitted court review of union actions against individual members and required unions to adopt standards for internal conduct and financial control.

The Landrum-Griffin Act defines member rights, requires the adoption of a written constitution and bylaws, regulates the use of trusteeship (when the national union "takes over" a local), sets election standards, and permits union members to sue their leaders for breaches of fiduciary responsibility, when union leaders misuse union funds. The Landrum-Griffin Act did not produce the predicted widespread membership participation in union affairs or expose massive union corruption. The workers' "Bill of Rights" may have encouraged more candidates for local union office and did result in more uniform financial accounting procedures. Dissident union members are now protected from arbitrary disciplinary proceedings, sometimes encouraging more spirited national union elections.

Since the passage of the Civil Rights Act (1964), the courts have gone even further. Not only must the union abide by its own constitution and rules, the rules themselves must be reasonable and may not contravene the U.S. Constitution. The courts have held that even the union shop, which makes continued union membership a condition of employment, delegates enough power to the union to require that internal disciplinary procedures rely on due process and impartial arbitrators.

Court decisions have established minimal levels of procedure for regulating leadership-membership interaction. Some individual unions have gone further. In 1957, the UAW began an outside review process which included nonunion neutrals to review the conduct of internal union affairs. The AFL-CIO investigates charges of corruption within individual unions, but its powers are limited to publicity and expulsion. The AFL-CIO sanction is typically not decisive.

Most union leaders are former workers who were also union activists. The tendency to promote from within increases leadership sensitivity to workplace concerns, but raises a select few persons to a wage far in excess of that obtained while working. Unions with 100,000 or more members typically pay their presidents an annual salary of at least $40,000 and provide a (smaller) expense account—giving the former worker an income and status which can be enjoyed, in most instances, only with continued office tenure.[7] The result is a continual pressure to retain power, with the leader often using the "need for internal unity" approach to stifle dissent. Until unions provide alternatives to former officials in, for example, the labor colleges which train local leaders, pressure for continued tenure will remain.

The proper relationship between union leaders and union membership recalls the perennial "union democracy" issue. How democratic are unions?

---

[7]Most union leaders are careful not to allow their salaries to escalate too much above average member incomes. The president of the machinists' union, for example, received a salary of only $41,000 for representing 700,000 machinists in 1975. The Teamsters, in contrast, provided President F. E. Fitzsimmons a salary of $125,000, dwarfing even the $90,000 paid to George Meany.

How democratic should unions be? Must the internal behavior of unions reflect the ideals of political democracy, or is the primary role of the union to inject democracy into the workplace by acting as a countervailing force to management? The union democracy issue is as old as the labor movement, and remains the subject of debate today.

Labor law requires certain (minimal) "forms" of union democracy; that is, unions must have constitutions, conduct honest elections for leaders, hold regular meetings, and rely on due process procedures for meting out fines and discipline. Even if union conduct conforms to legal requirements, are union members afforded a "reasonable" voice in decision making? Many observers point to low attendance at local union meetings, the lack of contested (national) union elections, and waning interest in union-sponsored activities as evidence of the lack of union democracy. But such criticism is often misguided. A better-educated labor force usually has more alternative uses of free time and, if a few workers *do* attend union meetings, those attending can report the results back to their fellow workers. The absence of contested elections may indicate either satisfaction or lack of democracy, but neither can be inferred directly from this circumstance. Finally, if a more sophisticated labor force comes to view the union as a workplace advocate, why should the individual want to bring union activities into his personal life? Attendance at union meetings increases sharply before bargaining and during strikes, making the maintenance of labor peace, a primary social objective, also responsible for an apparent decline in union meeting attendance.

The American labor movement is becoming concerned about a widely perceived negative public image. This image, derived in part by the growing gulf between the affluent unionized work force and others in the labor force, occurs at a time of renewed intraunion disputes. Contested national union elections, once rare, are becoming more common; and the tactics used by incumbents and challengers often court public disfavor. A reform-minded candidate for the presidency of the United Mine Workers (UMW), Joseph Yablonski, was murdered in an attempt to unseat the established incumbent, W. A. ("Tony") Boyle. Another reform candidate, Arnold Miller, eventually unseated Boyle, but found himself accused of inept administration and a disregard for certain union rules while being reelected in 1977. National leadership contests expose similarities between big unions and big business leaders. Ed Sadlowski, a militant director of the Chicago Steelworkers district, challenged Lloyd McBride, an "establishment" USW leader, in another 1977 election. Although defeated, Sadlowski's charges of "tuxedo unionism"—union leaders who "think and act like businessmen"—helped reinforce a public image of organized labor which sees unions as apologists for a labor elite.

Although the AFL-CIO has a formidable lobbying organization and makes significant campaign contributions through its Committee On Political Education (COPE), its legislative setbacks in 1976 and 1977 have renewed calls for a rejuvenation within the labor movement. Unions will make new efforts to organize workers in southern and rural plants, while the AFL-CIO presses for welfare reform and national health insurance—programs designed to benefit more people outside unions than in them. It is too soon to judge the success of these moves to refurbish labor's image; but it must be remembered that calls for a return to militant rank-and-file, or member-oriented, unionism are periodic, not an event first prompted by events of the 1970s.

Union-Management Organizational Differences

Collective bargaining is a relationship between organizations. Since the structure of an organization does much to explain organizational power and performance, a brief explanation of differences between business and union organizations is in order.

The crucial difference between unions and management organizations is the political-democratic nature of the union but the hierarchic-authoritarian nature of business. Unions elect officials, solicit bargaining demands from the membership, and frequently require the membership to vote on any agreement reached. Although union leaders can sometimes manipulate members, most unions are organized as a pyramid with the ultimate check on power at the bottom, in the union membership. Management, in contrast, is organized to allow defined authority relationships. Managers are appointed, not elected; and each has defined powers and responsibilities. Although management can be removed by stockholders, the threat is usually more pressing from those within the management hierarchy than from the distant owners of capital.

Organizational differences become most apparent in bargaining and negotiation, where information and time are critical. Union leaders package an array of demands with (confidential) priorities attached to each. Management responds to the union-initiated demands, and the give-and-take constitutes the negotiation process. But while management representatives can be given objective negotiation guidelines (e.g., do not concede more than 10 percent in total labor costs), the union leader is aware that the resulting agreement must be "sold to the membership" when making concessions. If, for example, management refuses to yield on a certain work condition demand which affects only a part of the work force, the union leadership must obtain an offsetting concession or risk a membership revolt. Union leaders can, of course, make quick judgments if they are secure in their position or are in close touch with workplace concerns.

Summary

National (or international) unions are composed of building-block locals. National unions—the key units in the American labor movement—are, in turn, federated into the AFL-CIO. The AFL-CIO is an association of national unions;

it has no voice in collective bargaining, which is done within each national union. Although four in five union members are associated with an AFL-CIO union, the two largest national unions—the Teamsters and the Auto Workers—remain outside the federation.

Unions collects dues and initiation fees, generating $3.5 billion annually. The administrative inexperience of (especially local) union officials makes some unions ripe for financial malfeasance. Although union corruption does exist, its incidence is relatively rare. The Landrum-Griffin Act (1959) forced unions to disclose their financial dealings and made it easier for union members to oppose existent leadership.

Unions are nominally political-democratic bodies, while businesses are organized along hierarchic-authoritarian lines. The need for union leaders to "sell" any contract negotiated to the membership forces union leaders to be very conscious of true member feelings or risk a membership revolt. Because union leaders must weigh the consequences of particular bargaining tradeoffs for different groups of workers, unions typically react more slowly during the negotiation process than managements.

Bibliography

Barbash, J. *American Unions: Structure, Government, and Politics.* New York: Random House, 1967.

An excellent introduction to union organization and administration.

Industrial Relations 16: 2 (May, 1977).

Contains a symposium on research into union structure and government.

James, Ralph, and Estelle James. *Hoffa and the Teamsters: A Study of Union Power.* Princeton, N.J.: D. Van Nostrand, 1965.

The intriguing story of how one union leader, largely by force of personality, was able to centralize bargaining in the trucking industry.

Leiserson, W. *American Trade Union Democracy.* New York: Columbia University Press, 1959.

A review prompted by the charges of corruption in labor unions.

Taft, P. *The Structure and Government of Labor Unions.* Cambridge, Mass.: Harvard University Press, 1954.

Dated, but a good description of the evolution of union structure.

The Collective Bargaining Interaction

6

The process of industrialization fundamentally altered the structure of society, producing competing classes of disruptive, profit-seeking entrepreneurs and dependent, security-conscious workers. Entrepreneurs require workers who, in turn, become dependent on them for income-earning opportunities. When workers exchange effort for income, employer and worker interests collide; as employers attempt to secure labor as cheaply as possible, workers seek to maximize their income and security. These conflicting interests must be resolved before production can actually occur. Since production is the event necessary to benefit both employers and workers, employers and workers have incentives to minimize conflict, to cooperate rather than engage in conflict. The clash between efficiency and security is continual, forcing workers and employers to resolve conflicts continually rather than holding only periodic negotiations. Collective bargaining is the "tool" of labor relations which is used to resolve conflict and promote cooperation, to assure labor peace rather than labor strife.

An inherent feature of work in modern society is this inevitable conflict of interest (and the need for cooperation) between worker and employer. But *union*-employer conflict is not. Unions represent only a fraction of the labor force, confining transactions between organized groups of workers and employer(s) to a subset of those occurring in everyday life.[1] To accommodate the inherent conflicts between organized workers and employers, a variety of instruments is available to unions, including political actions, pressures for participation in management, or bargaining over wages and working conditions. Collective bargaining is only one of the instruments available to unions in their quest for legitimacy and accommodation. In America, collective bargaining has become the central purpose of unions and is the primary instrument through which employers and unions settle their differences.

---

[1]It should be noted that unions, although representing only about 20 percent of all workers, typically exert a disproportionate influence on prevailing wages and working conditions. Many companies forestall unionization by matching or bettering union contracts, and, in a few instances, public policy legally extends union rates to nonunion employers (e.g., the Davis-Bacon Act makes "prevailing wages," usually union rates, those which must be paid on federal construction projects). In Europe, contract extension is more common, a point we return to later in this chapter.

Collective bargaining is an interaction between a group of workers and an employer or employers. Elected or appointed worker representatives meet and confer with management representatives to negotiate an agreement covering "the employment relationship." Before meaningful interaction can occur, there must be some understanding of each side's needs and some mutual desire for an eventual agreement. If the employer refuses to share *any* power or if the union views the employer as an "illegitimate capitalist," no basis for mutual accommodation exists, since it would be heretical to sign a contract with a nonentity. Throughout history, many employers refused to concede any meaningful voice to unions, and some unions refused to sign contracts with capitalists, preventing the negotiation and compromise so characteristic of collective bargaining. The history of trade unionism is largely the story of how this foundation of legitimacy and accommodation was erected to permit recognition and maintain a relationship between unions and employers.

Collective bargaining did not arrive with the early trade unions. Initially, "bargaining" consisted of the employer's posting a wage schedule (often a wage cut) or the union's promulgating its wage demands. Each party acted unilaterally, the union striking and picketing to demonstrate dissatisfaction and the employer resorting to lockouts or strikebreakers. Communication was sporadic at best, often occurring in the heated atmosphere of a picket line rather than during normal discussions. The use of posted wage offers and unilateral actions instead of discussion and shared decision making persisted well into the twentieth century.

Contemporary collective bargaining begins from an established framework, defined by traditions, economic forces, and public policies expressed in a variety of labor laws and regulations. Bargaining occurs when unions and management seek to negotiate new agreements or revise expiring ones; when labor agreements are administered through a complaint-and-resolution or grievance mechanism; and when joint employer-union committees consult on safety, technology, or some other issue of mutual concern. Since there is no "right" outcome in any of these negotiations, agreement is reached by threatening to use the weapons from the arsenal each side possesses. The "biggest guns" are the union strike and picket, countered by the management lockout and striker replacement. The strike and lockout impose costly burdens on both sides and, in practice, they are usually reserved for disputes over *interests* in contract negotiation. Complaints or grievances arising from the *rights* granted in an existing agreement can usually be appealed to a neutral arbitrator, and the joint committees work to arrive at solutions to problems before they erupt into complaints and strikes. The process is both complex and continuous. Union and management representatives may be in daily contact to resolve the issues which arise every workday.

The focus of contemporary collective bargaining is the written agreement, the "treaty" between union and management which binds both parties to a mutually agreeable set of rights and obligations while the agreement is in force. Although collective bargaining is concerned with all matters affecting "the employment relationship,'' two terms of employment are prominent in American labor agreements: (1) the price of labor, that is, the wage and fringe benefit package, and (2) the conditions of labor's sale, or the work rules which govern rights and duties in the workplace. When union and management seek to write a new contract or revise an existing one, they are bargaining to accommodate conflicting interests. After agreement is reached, rights (under the agreement) are established, rights which must be interpreted and defined on a continuing basis in the workplace. The collective bargaining system centers on the written agreement, first on the procedures for establishing agreement and then on the day-to-day interpretation of it.

In this chapter, we view collective bargaining from economic and organizational perspectives. The first section outlines the collective bargaining framework. Bargaining is a process of negotiation and compromise (''higgling,'' to use the Webbs' term), a process influenced by economic, organizational, and legal factors. As negotiations proceed, each side employs strategies and tactics to force concessions. Usually, offer and counteroffer result in agreement. If an impasse exists, the parties sometimes invoke weapons which inflict damage on the adversary, the union strike countered by the management lockout or the replacement of striking workers. The ''power'' each side possesses in bargaining helps determine both tactics and the shape of any final agreement. In the concluding section, we examine several theories of bargaining power. The law governing employer-employee relationships as well as the administration of the collective bargaining agreement are treated in Chapter 7.

The Bargaining Framework

Collective bargaining is a procedure through which an employer or employers can negotiate agreements covering wages and working conditions with employee representatives. Workers are represented by an appointed or elected bargaining team while employer representation depends on the size of the organization and its degree of specialization. In smaller operations, the company president may be involved in bargaining, while larger companies have separate industrial relations departments. Since World War II, both unions and employers have come to view bargaining as a specialized function, providing bargainers with economic and legal research assistants. The resulting ''professionalism'' in bargaining often makes it appear less a worker-employer clash, as bargaining professionals have made the process far more rational.

Union and management representatives meet to ''higgle'' over the terms of a new or expiring agreement. In smaller operations, bargaining may occur in a company conference room, but unions usually press for a neutral site (a hotel, motel, or conference center) to avoid the psychological advantage handed employers in their own facilities. Negotiation or higgling continues until agreement is reached on three broad sets of issues: compensation, job rights, and grievance procedures.[2] After informal agreement is reached, the parties reduce the agreement to written form, a process which often requires further negotiation until mutually acceptable wording is found. The agreement continues in force for a specified period, usually two or three years, until it expires and a new agreement is negotiated. Most collective bargaining sessions today involve the renegotiation of expiring contracts, not negotiation of a first agreement.

Collective bargaining is a power-based relationship (each side can inflict costs on the other) among a variety of organizations, from a building contractor with two employees to an industrial giant with 200,000. The variety of industries and employers makes it necessary to determine the appropriate **bargaining unit** for bargaining. Which employees will a particular union represent—all workers in a plant, only those with certain skills, all workers in a given geographic area, or all the workers of a single company or industry? Although the possibilities appear numerous, most bargaining units are determined by tradition, logic, and comparison with other industries—if the auto workers usually organize by plant, then the bargaining unit will be the entire plant's work force. If disputes arise, the National Labor Relations Board (NLRB) is empowered to determine an appropriate bargaining unit.

After a union has been certified as the bargaining representative for a group of workers, it becomes the *exclusive* agent for those workers in matters relating to wages, hours, and conditions of employment. This "exclusivity" means that there is only one union per bargaining unit (e.g., only the UAW to represent production workers in an auto plant). In Europe, by contrast, it is common to find several unions representing the same type of worker (e.g., production workers) in a plant (e.g., in France, separate Communist and Socialist unions representing auto assembly workers) or a variety of unions each representing a particular craft, as in Britain. American exclusivity is usually an asset in bargaining—while the European unions form (often uneasy) coalitions for bargaining, the American union is free from the threat that rival unions may appear more militant or more successful.

The exclusivity of American bargaining also affects the ability of the individual to bargain directly with the employer. The Webbs, who viewed collective bargaining as one of many union instruments (rather than the central purpose of unions), saw collective bargaining as the antithesis of individual bargaining.

> The individual workman, applying for a job, accepts or refuses the terms offered by the employer without communication with his fellow workmen [. . . driving] a strictly individual bargain. But if a group of workmen concert together, and send representatives to conduct the bargaining on behalf

---

[2]A fourth set of issues mandating agreement, those governing collective relations or the rights of the trade union as an organization, are usually established in the first contract and do not require renegotiation each time bargaining occurs.

of the whole body, the position is at once changed. Instead of the employer making a series of separate contracts with isolated individuals, he meets a collective will, and settles, in a single agreement, the principles upon which, for the time being, all workmen of a particular group, class, or grade will be engaged.[3]

For the Webbs, collective bargaining was merely the aggregation of individual bargaining powers, that is, the formation of a labor cartel. If some workers were to engage in individual bargaining (because they had, for instance, specific skills), the bargaining power of the group would be diminished.

As we shall see, the analogy between individual and collective bargaining is somewhat misleading. Although an individual contract typically applies to a specific person and details wages and conditions for him/her, a collective agreement does not apply to any particular individual. The collective agreement specifies the rules which govern the hiring, payment, and firing of individuals, but it does not name particular individuals as an individual contract would. In many ways, collective bargaining is more of a rule-making process, since a negotiated wage is meaningless without reference to the work rules under which it is earned.[4] Although economic power affects the division of benefits arising from the rules, the collective agreement provides no economic benefits to specific individuals, it merely dictates the terms under which any individual who works must be employed. Individual bargaining is permitted under Section 9(a) of the Taft-Hartley Act, but its usage is largely confined to those sectors where the union negotiates minimum wages and the ''stars'' obtain additional individual benefits, as in professional sports and acting. Most collective bargaining agreements are too detailed and localized to leave subjects for individual bargaining.

After determining who is to be the exclusive bargaining agent for a particular group of workers, the parties must determine the scope of bargaining, that is, the range of issues which are bargainable. The law provides some guidance by distinguishing mandatory, permissive, and proscribed bargaining subjects, but these distinctions are often blurred if one party has enough bargaining power to force the subject to be considered. Most agreements begin with an identification of the parties and definitions of union and management rights (Table 6.1).

Union security is augmented by a dues **checkoff** system, found in 95 percent of all agreements, through which the employer deducts union dues from wages and forwards the monies to the union. Many agreements go further, establishing the agency (or union) shop, which requires dues payment (or union membership) as a condition of continued employment after a thirty-day probation. Some union security clauses go further, requiring the employer, for exam-

---

[3]Sidney and Beatrice Webb, *Industrial Democracy* (London: Longmans, 1902), p. 178.

[4]For an elaboration of this theory of bargaining, see A. Flanders, ''Collective Bargaining: A Theoretical Analysis,'' *British Journal of Industrial Relations* 6: 1 (March, 1968): 1–26.

Table 6.1 Major Labor Contract Provisions

1. Union Security and Management Rights Clauses
    Definitions and identification of parties
    Union security and dues checkoff
    Management rights
    Antidiscrimination clauses
    Safety and productivity committees
    Absenteeism and tardiness

2. Wages and Related Provisions
    Wage administration
    Methods of compensation
    Rate structure
    Profit sharing, stock purchases, and bonuses
    Incentive pay and shift differentials

3. Hours of Work and Overtime Pay
    Scheduled daily and weekly hours
    Weekend hours
    Overtime pay
    Allocation of overtime hours

4. Paid and Unpaid Leave
    Vacations and holidays
    Leaves of absence (for military service, maternity, and so on)
    Time for union business

5. Employee Benefits
    Health insurance plans
    Pension plans

6. Seniority
    Seniority lists
    Probationary periods
    Retention of seniority rights

7. Job Security Clauses
    Work rules
    Supplemental unemployment benefits
    Subcontracting
    Apprenticeship and training
    Severance pay and transfer rights

8. Dispute Settlement
    Grievance procedures
    Arbitration and mediation
    Strikes and lockouts
    Contract enforcement

Source: Adapted from U.S. Department of Labor, *Characteristics of Major Collective Bargaining Agreements* (Washington, D.C.: U.S. Government Printing Office, 1975).

ple, to give preference to union members when hiring. Management rights clauses typically reserve for management all powers and prerogatives not constrained by law or the agreement, while antidiscrimination clauses and joint committees work to ensure fair treatment and promote employer-union cooperation.

The wage and hour provisions of labor agreements get most publicity. The agreements specify the compensation scheme, including general wage levels and wage differentials, any incentive or bonus plans, and compensation for vacations, holidays, and sick leave. Scheduled work hours are detailed, as are provisions for overtime, weekend, and holiday work. In most of these provisions, it is the *method* of allocating work which is negotiated, not the actual number of hours or the amount of overtime. Scheduled wage levels are supplemented by an expanding package of employee fringe benefits, including health insurance and pension plans.

The job rights sections of the labor agreement are among the most important to individual workers. Those job rights describe hiring, promotion and transfer, and layoff procedures, detailing the computation and applicability of seniority rights. Work rules or plant operations clauses establish the work rules which govern rest periods, shift schedules, and discipline and discharge procedures, while job security clauses govern work subcontracting, any supplemental unemployment benefits, and severance pay.

Collective bargaining agreements often conclude with dispute settlement provisions, detailing the procedures for filing and appealing grievances and invoking arbitration, requiring notice of intended strikes or lockouts, and making provisions for enforcement of the contract. If necessary, the parties can agree to make special provisions for particular (groups of) workers, including union representatives, older workers, apprentices, and women and minority workers. A copy of the resulting agreement (up to 300 pages in autos and steel) is usually provided to each worker.

Each of the various subjects of bargaining can quickly assume a complexity which slows progress toward agreement. Many of the contingencies which do arise can be resolved through grievance procedures, but others, including the ever-expanding fringe benefit package, require agreement at the outset of a contract period. The increased complexity of bargaining has accentuated a trend toward larger bargaining units. Unions which once bargained on a plant-by-plant basis may seek to enlarge the bargaining unit to cover all workers in a company's plants, shifting bargaining from a plant to a companywide basis. In such bargaining, companywide agreements are often supplemented by plant negotiations, but the basic contract is established at the more inclusive company level. Similarly, local (craft) unions often combine on a city or regional basis, negotiating a "master" agreement which serves to guide the individual unions in supplemental bargaining.

Unions sometimes favor more inclusive bargaining units. Larger bargaining units can increase the union's bargaining power (especially when the union can completely shut down a particular company) while they promote company or industrywide uniformity of wages and working conditions, a standardization often sought by both unions and employers. If the union bargains over complex issues for many workers, it may be more ready to utilize outside experts in contract negotiations, since their cost can be spread over more workers. Larger bargaining units also increase the power of union leaders, since union power is concentrated where basic negotiations are conducted. In the most celebrated recent example, Jimmy Hoffa was able to centralize his power as Teamster's president by shifting bargaining in the trucking industry from the local and regional level to the level of a national agreement.[5]

Unions sometimes press for industrywide **multiemployer bargaining units,** but employers often resist.[6] Some employers, reluctant to surrender decision-making power to unions, may also resist wage concessions other employers are willing to concede. Most employers prefer to rely on their own bargaining strengths, unencumbered by the needs of particularly strong or weak rivals in a multiemployer bargaining unit. Although multiemployer bargaining units are exempted from antitrust laws, some employers still fear government intervention to influence a settlement or avoid a strike. If the union negotiates a "pattern agreement" with the dominant firm in an industry, its smaller rivals may plead economic hardship and seek more favorable terms from the union, rather than being locked in by a uniform multiemployer agreement.

Despite an ebb and flow of opinion by both unions and management, the number of large bargaining units has been increasing in America. Employers find that multiemployer units may prevent "whipsaw strikes," where the union plays one company off against another, and give smaller companies a direct voice in the final agreement. Some unions have lost enthusiasm for larger bargaining units because they keep the union from extracting all it could from particularly profitable companies, but the union's desire for industrywide standardization usually overcomes the pressure to provide advantages to favored workers which could result from company-by-company negotiations.

Although there is a trend toward consolidation of bargaining units, collective bargaining remains very decentralized. In 1974, for example, some 175,000 collective bargaining agreements were in force, covering the nations's 21.6 million unionized workers. Most of these agreements are single employer agreements, negotiated between a local (of a national) union and covering a single plant or workplace. Only about 2,000 agreements are considered "major agreements," covering 1,000 or more workers. Most major agreements are negotiated by national unions and a single employer with several plants or a group of employers. A single union may make a number of agreements; in 1974, some thirty-two unions had 1,000 or more agreements each. Over time, the concentration of agreements in the hands of a few unions is increasing— two thirds of all collective bargaining agreements are made by unions having at least 5,000 agreements.

---

[5]For the fascinating story of Hoffa's acquisition and use of union power, see Ralph and Estelle James, *Hoffa and the Teamsters: A Study in Union Power.* (Princeton, N.J.: D. Van Nostrand, 1965). Since the demise of Hoffa, bargaining in the trucking industry has reverted to the regional and local levels, as restless regional and local leaders successfully pushed for a return of their old bargaining powers.

[6]In some industries, such as construction, *employers* press for more inclusive bargaining units to counter the union's power to whipsaw (to strike only one contractor but continue working for a competitor). In other industries, such as airlines, this union tactic has produced employer mutual aid pacts, through which nonstruck employers make up the losses of the employer experiencing a strike.

Decentralized bargaining is peculiar to the United States and Canada. In Europe, for example, employer associations to promote cooperation have a long history. Smaller markets permitted fewer large companies, and less competition (as well as an absence of strict antitrust laws) resulted in employer cooperation even before the advent of trade unionism. When unions made their impact in the early 1900s, these employer associations became natural bodies to prevent unions from playing one company off against another. European employer associations typically have far more control over their member companies than do American bargaining associations, often making key lockout decisions and enforcing member employer compliance.

European employers are more willing to accept the discipline of the association because they are often covered by a negotiated agreement even if they are not association members. After unions and employers negotiate an agreement covering at least 50 percent of the work force in any industry or occupation, the Ministry of Labor is empowered to ''extend to agreement'' throughout the industry or occupation in France, Germany, Belgium, Austria, and Switzerland.[7] Given union movements which often see the whole working class as their natural constituency, even if they represent only a fraction of the workers, the role of associations and the practice of contract extension broadens the scope of already inclusive European bargaining units to industrywide or even national levels.[8]

The Negotiation Process

Negotiation is the process of conferring to reach a settlement of conflicting claims. In labor relations, negotiation occurs in the periodic meetings between labor and management representatives to renegotiate collective bargaining agreements. Negotiations only result in settlement if both sides have a ''will to agreement,'' if the consequences of not agreeing are worse than the impacts of the agreement. The negotiator deploys an array of strategies and tactics—a long list of (outrageous) demands, bluffs to conceal true priorities, selected concessions, and finally agreement or use of the threatened weapon to force agreement.

---

[7]The best American example of such "extension" practices is in the construction industry. The Davis-Bacon Act (1931), passed in an era of wage cuts, sought to keep the federal government from "depressing local wage conditions" by requiring that contractors bidding on government construction projects agree to pay wages and fringes at least equivalent to the levels "prevailing" in the locality. In practice, the Secretary of Labor has usually found union standards to be the "prevailing standards," thus extending union negotiated wages and fringes to the nonunion labor force on government construction projects.

[8]One reason American labor agreements would be hard to extend is their localized detail. In Europe, industrywide or national agreements are often quite general, permitting some scope for local supplements. But American agreements are detailed, reflecting the conditions of a particular company or group of companies. It would be much more difficult to extend the detailed American agreement to noncovered companies than it is the general European agreement.

The outcome of the negotiating process is important for several reasons. Negotiations which result in settlements do not disrupt the production of goods or the provision of services, permitting economic continuity. But negotiated outcomes also serve to reward workers for their efforts. If agreement is imposed, by governmental fiat or indirectly through persuasion, worker dissatisfaction may impair production efficiency over the two- or three-year life of the agreement. Although it may be desirable to limit the discontinuities accompanying a work stoppage in the short term, it must be remembered that the absence of an actual work stoppage does not guarantee peaceful and productive labor relations.

Most union-management negotiations today merely serve to revise an expiring contract. Since bargaining "maturity" is often reached only after each side gains some understanding of the other's problems and priorities, contemporary collective bargaining is more rational than that which occurs during the "first negotiations," when the employer is first surrendering a share of his management prerogatives and the union is flush with an election victory, often achieved after promises of an array of new benefits. The key difference between the first agreement and subsequent revisions is the fact that, after an agreement exists, negotiations can proceed from a written, formerly agreed-upon document. From 1972 through 1974, about 10,000 agreements were negotiated for the first time; the remaining 165,000 were either renegotiated or in force over the two-year period.[9] Since most negotiations are for agreement revision, the concept of "renegotiation," rather than first contract negotiation, is most accurate.

Under the National Labor Relations Act, any party wishing to change a collective bargaining agreement must give the other party notice at least sixty days prior to the expiration date of the agreement. In most instances, the union takes the initiative in proposing a series of additions, deletions, or changes in the expiring agreement. The company may make a completely independent counterproposal or respond by offering alternatives to each union suggestion. Even before negotiations begin, the union has solicited and presented a list of demands and the company has given its initial reaction to the union suggestions.

The simplest form of negotiation is to take the existing agreement and merely alter the compensation terms (and perhaps some work rules) in accord with the parties' own needs or in light of some other "pattern-setting" agreement. Since most of the agreements cover relatively few workers (e.g., 50 or 100), neither side expects negotiations to be conducted in expensive rented facilities for weeks or months. Both the union and the employer are aware of

---

[9]Data on the number of collective bargaining agreements are not without ambiguity. These figures were derived from the U.S. Department of Labor's *Directory of National Unions and Employer Associations, 1975* (Washington, D.C.: U.S. Government Printing Office, 1977), pp. 77–78.

the terms reached in "major agreements," and negotiations establish the extent to which the small employer will conform to the pattern agreement.

Negotiation of major or pattern agreements is more complicated. To re-negotiate these contracts (covering 725,000 auto workers, for example), negotiators and economists on each side appraise the company's economic performance and prospects. The union negotiating committee solicits bargaining proposals from the rank and file, especially wage demands and desired rule changes. Lawyers prepare alternative "contract language" documents which translate union and company demands into final form. For most major agreements, preparation for biennial or triennial negotiations begins a year or more in advance, and often utilizes the services of specialists to bolster a bargaining position, especially on the union side.

Most negotiating lists contain three sets of demands. The whole list of union demands (and the employer's counteroffer) is the "shopping list," which includes many "unrealistic" items demanded by workers and presented to demonstrate the union's representation role. This public list is a far cry from the final settlement, prompting many outsiders to question the necessity of a ritual involving nonachievable demands, but the list does serve to permit individuals to voice their demands and serves as a starting point for negotiations. Even before negotiations begin, each party attempts to determine: (1) what is the minimum package necessary, and (2) what are the real priorities among the long list of demands on the negotiating table?

Union bargaining teams solicit worker desires during the life of the agreement and at special preparation-for-bargaining meetings. The formation of management bargaining goals is more ambiguous, in part because management typically *responds* to union-initiated demands. The determination of maximum management financial concessions rests with the financial staff, while responses to work rule and plant operation demands are formulated after discussions with production management and line supervisors. If any particular rule has resulted in a rash of grievances, management will seek modification or elimination of the source of discontent.

In addition to internally generated demands and needs, both union and management bargaining teams prepare for negotiation by examining industry- or economywide trends in economic and noneconomic benefits. Data derived from government reports on trends in wages and fringes may be utilized to bolster a union demand or provide a basis for management resistance. Both parties pay particular attention to the results of negotiations in similar negotiations. Union leaders are well aware of their "orbits of coercive comparison," or industries and unions with whom the membership expects benefit equality. Management is sensitive to the outcomes of competitor negotiations, since it must compete with its rivals in the product market. Unions and management take preparations for bargaining very seriously, since demands justified by facts and logic are far more effective than arguments which appeal to rhetoric or ideology.

Negotiation is the art of compromise, of conceding at one point to achieve agreement elsewhere, or, in one expert's words, "an exercise in graceful retreat—retreating without seeming to retreat.''[10] Priorities and minimum demands are disguised, forcing the bargaining parties to parry as they fend off questions and demands aimed at exposing primary and secondary demands. Both parties have a good idea of the ultimate ''settlement range,'' those wage and fringe benefit packages which it is more rational to accept than to resort to strikes or lockouts. The tone and ultimate outcome of the bargaining process depend on the economic (bargaining power) situation, the degree of labor-management rapport, the personalities of the negotiators, outside events, and bargaining strategies and tactics. Most negotiations include an initial testing and jockeying stage, during which the parties explain demands to each other without making commitments or asserting priorities, followed by a period of consolidation, during which some agreements and tradeoffs become apparent. As the ritual proceeds, demands are repackaged, with the union, for example, backing off a demand for longer rest periods in exchange for a wage increase of five cents an hour. The negotiating language often conceals true differences, with union ''no contract, no work'' statements countered by management's variations on ''this is our final offer'' or ''this is the limit we can concede to remain competitive.''

Before either side resorts to strikes or lockouts, the third stage of negotiation begins. The range of issues has been narrowed as well as the differences between the parties. The union may set a strike date if agreement is not reached, and outside mediators may be called in to promote agreement. It is in this crisis atmosphere that name calling and ''nonrealistic'' language abounds. Despite the apocalyptic language, most negotiations result in agreement *before* the existing contract expires.[11] After an informal agreement is reached, lawyers reduce the agreement to its legal, written form.

Agreement between negotiators does not end the bargaining process. In most unions, the negotiated agreement must be ratified by a majority of the union members covered. If the union negotiators have conceded too much, union members may reject the agreement despite the negotiator's plea that it ''represents the best we can do.'' Although some rejections are ''staged'' by union leaders to augment their bargaining power (the rejection allows them to return to the bargaining table and make renewed efforts on particular subjects), an increasing percentage (now 5 to 10 percent) of negotiated agreements are rejected on the first ratification vote. Some observers point to the increased frequency of contract rejection as evidence that union leaders are ''out of touch'' with their members, but it appears that most rejections result from more mundane communication failures within the union.

---

[10]Clark Kerr, ''Bargaining Processes,'' in E. Bakke, C. Kerr, and C. Anrod (eds.), *Unions, Management and the Public* (New York: Harcourt Brace Jovanovich, 1967), p. 307.

[11]The negotiator's skill is often derived from an ability to remain mindful of the ultimate settlement range despite the required rhetoric. Union negotiators who too flippantly announce ''no contract, no work'' may be forced into a humble retreat if a strike requires picketing in mid-winter cold. Similarly, ''final offers'' are often subject to humiliating change, when a skillful concession forces the company negotiator to change the ''final offer'' to avoid a strike.

To avoid the crisis atmosphere of many negotiations, when both parties are striving to reach agreement before the contract expires, some industries have experimented with "continuous bargaining." The most prominent example of such bargaining is in the steel industry. Although the last strike was in 1959, buyers of steel began stockpiling steel and placing orders with foreign producers to forestall shortages in the event of a strike. The result was steelworker unemployment for two reasons—even though the unions did *not* strike, massive layoffs still occurred, until steel users were able to work off their inventories. In addition, each threatened strike increased steel customers' reliance on foreign suppliers, causing permanent job losses. As one steel executive noted, both sides "were enduring the penalties of strikes even though we didn't have them."[12]

In 1973, the United Steelworkers of America and the ten basic steel producers signed an Experimental Negotiating Agreement (ENA). The ENA called for negotiations to proceed as usual, but provided for outside arbitration of any disputed *interests* (rather than a strike) not settled by the contract expiration date.[13] The ENA's "continuous bargaining" achieved agreement on virtually all issues without resorting to arbitration during the 1974 and 1977 negotiations. Although some union members viewed the surrender of the right to strike a heresy, union officers who supported the ENA were elected in 1977. Because both parties are reluctant to permit an "outsider" to impose a *contract* settlement, continuous bargaining and no-strike clauses have not spread rapidly, but they may serve useful purposes in industries subject to demand fluctuations or foreign competition.

The cooperative spirit of continuous bargaining requires a high degree of union-employer trust. Each side must understand and respect the needs of its bargaining adversary. In 1977, the United Steelworkers union negotiated a "rule of 65" which fostered early retirement by increasing pensions for any worker (with at least twenty years of service) whose age plus years of employment added to sixty-five or more. Steel demand weakened, and the steel companies began closing "obsolete" steel mills. In November and December of 1977, just before the "rule of 65" became effective (January 1, 1978), some 7,300 steelworkers were discharged by Bethlehem Steel. Of those discharged, 821 would have been eligible for the increased pension benefits. The company argued that it was not required to pay benefits because the contract provision was not yet in force, while the union held that workers discharged in similar situations in the past were entitled to such promised benefits. Although an arbi-

---

[12]Quoted in P. Shabecoff, "Growth of Arbitration Appears to Point to Era of Labor Peace," *New York Times,* April 22, 1973, p. 46.

[13]It should be noted that *local* unions retain the right to strike over local issues. The first such major strikes occurred among USW members in the Minnesota iron-ore range in 1977. The strike persisted for several months, as unions and management disputed whether the issue of local incentive pay was a local issue, and therefore subject to strike action, or a national issue, which must be submitted to binding arbitration.

tration panel eventually upheld the union position, the dispute generated enough union-employer conflict to threaten the unraveling of the ENA.

Some of the interest in strike alternatives results from the increasing influence of government in the outcome of the bargaining process. Until unions were legally protected in 1935, public policy had supported the idea of employer unilateralism in employment, which left the employer free to make decisions about wages, working conditions, and discharge without public interference.[14] The enactment of labor relations legislation in the 1930s changed the government attitude—public policy now required employers to meet with bargaining representatives and attempt to reach agreement, making employment decisions bilateral (between union and employer) rather than the sole prerogative of the employer. Since the 1960s, public policy has expanded the number of decision makers once again. Federal wage-price controls or guidelines can limit the freedom of unions and management to set wages; affirmative action requirements can conflict with established hiring, promotion, and discharge procedures; and the government retains authority to halt strikes by obtaining "cooling-off" injunctions in national emergency situations. This "movement of the state from the periphery toward the center of the [collective bargaining] power relationship"[15] is the most significant new trend in private sector bargaining. Although its ramifications are not yet clear, it will limit the discretion of unions and management in making agreements as they attempt to accommodate a "third party" negotiator, the government.

Bargaining Power and the Bargaining Process

Negotiations toward agreement proceed because each side wishes to avoid the costs of the other's economic weapons, the union strike and the management lockout or striker replacement. But what determines relative union-management power to force concessions? What types of bargaining can be distinguished, and how do different kinds of bargaining affect relative power? In this section, we explore the concept of bargaining power—what it is, how it is obtained, and its use in collective bargaining.

In any situation where competing demands clash, the bargaining power of an adversary is the cost of disagreement. This cost of disagreement has two facets—it represents (1) the costs your adversary can impose on you and (2) the costs you can impose on your adversary. Your bargaining power is simply your ability to force agreement on your own terms, either by being able to impose

---

[14]Protective labor laws, constraining the employer's freedom of action in hiring women and children, were passed in the early 1900s. Protective labor laws, which protect workers by regulating employer conduct, can serve as bargaining floors, especially for low-paid workers.

[15]Jack Barbash, "The Changing Structure of Collective Bargaining," *Challenge*, September/October 1973, p. 45.

costs on others for disagreeing or by being willing to accept the costs which could be imposed on you.

The ideas behind individual bargaining power can be extended to conflicts between groups. New factors come into play, but the bargaining process begins with objective facts and attitudes and proceeds through a negotiating search. Since the search process can easily be visualized, a simple negotiation and search process is illustrated in Figure 6.1. Initial demands (shopping lists) are typically far apart, with the union demanding an expensive package and the employer offering very little. Both sides know the contract expiration date. After each negotiating session, the separate sides confer, and new proposals or counterproposals are offered (union bargaining power is usually vested in a committee, accounting for the discrete nature of union bargaining position changes but the more continuous nature of new management proposals, since management's bargaining power often rests with a single individual). If proposal and counterproposal meet, agreement is reached (note that concessions are more frequent as the contract expiration date nears). In the event that the parties are still "far apart" at contract time, a strike or lockout ensues, imposing costs on both parties.

Bargaining power, or the ability to move the opponent closer to *your* original demands, depends on a variety of factors. The most important set of influences are the facts of the situation—what are the company's profits? Its costs? Its market position? The state of the union is examined, and an assessment is made (by both sides) of the extent of internal unity, of probable assistance from other unions, and of the funds available to pay strike benefits. Although both sides can bluff, the ultimate power to force settlement largely depends on the economic and organizational facts of the respective parties.

In addition to facts, bargaining power is contingent on the actual demands made. Even a "powerful" union cannot force a doubling of wages overnight, limiting power to the "reasonableness" of demands. If the union or management can successfully bluff, causing the other party to underestimate its own power or overestimate an adversary's, agreement can be secured on more favorable terms than the "facts" would indicate. Finally, both sides seek to augment their bargaining power by making "no-cost" concessions. The union can agree to "cooperate" to increase efficiency or to be stricter with rule violators, and the company can promise to provide more information to the union or seek to reform particularly obnoxious supervisors. These no- or low-cost concessions often serve to "get negotiations moving" after a stalemate develops, and their skillful use means that a party can avoid making a "real" concession.

Given the divergence of initial positions and the tactics employed to seek concessions, the fact of eventual agreement may seem surprising. But both parties have a stake in reaching agreement, since the union can provide its members no benefits unless they work and the company earns no profit unless production occurs. Under some traditional mores, the relationship between unions and management was viewed as akin to a marriage agreement—individuals could disagree, even bitterly, but both had an overriding interest in

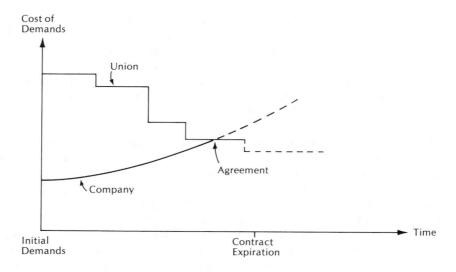

Figure 6.1. The Bargaining Process

eventually reaching agreement in order to continue the marriage. Changing social mores limit the usefulness of the analogy, since few union-management
disagreements result in dissolution of the company and the local union, but the
idea of a mutual need to reach agreement ultimately is the most powerful underlying force which constrains the use and abuse of bargaining power.

Over time, the relative bargaining power of unions and management is subject to change. Some view the post-World War II years as the peak of union
power, when industrial executives unsuccessfully sought to curb militant,
strike-prone unions. High unemployment and the Taft-Hartley Act curbed union
power from the mid-1950s until the military build-up of the 1960s. Since the
mid-sixties, the injection of government clouds an overall assessment of relative union or management power. In some private industries and sectors, notably trucking and longshoring, unions have successfully exerted their bargaining
power against coalitions of employers. But in other traditional union bastions,
including steel and autos, foreign competition and the construction of new
plants in the nonunion South have weakened traditionally strong unions. With
traditional manufacturing industries moving south and into rural areas, union
power is likely to be curtailed unless the new plants can be brought into the
union sphere of influence.

Although bargaining power shapes the outcome of negotiations, negotiations
actually consist of several distinct bargaining processes. At least four such bargaining processes can be distinguished: distributive bargaining, integrative bargaining, attitudinal structuring, and internal or intraorganizational bargaining.[16]

---

[16]R. Walton and R. McKinsie, *A Behavioral Theory of Labor Negotiations* (New York:
McGraw-Hill, 1965).

Each bargaining process is part of the negotiation procedure, and success in any phase helps shape the overall agreement.

The traditional collective bargaining model is the distributive, zero-sum game. In distributive bargaining, objectives conflict, as both sides view available resources as fixed and view concessions in a direct, "my loss is your gain" fashion. Since no "fair" or "normal" agreement is available, there is considerable room to bargain over the "fair" wage. In the absence of offsetting gains, the parties may view any wage increase as a benefit to the workers but simply an added cost to employers.

Rather than viewing available resources as fixed and higgling over union and management shares, integrative bargaining focuses on the shared objectives which promote a longer-term relationship between unions and management. After settling the basic wage package in a distributive fashion, unions and management can *cooperate* to select the best mode of delivering agreed-upon service, such as joint selection of a health or pension plan. Since the outcomes of integrative bargaining are often of a positive-sum nature, with both sides gaining from the agreement, integrative bargaining tends to be honest and frank, as each party specifies its true needs.

Unions and management also maintain a relationship after negotiations are concluded. Attitudinal structuring recognizes this need for postagreement cooperation, a cooperation vital when interpreting an often ambiguous agreement. If each side is distrustful of the other, a rash of grievances may result, imposing an outside arbitrator's decision because the parties have failed to agree. Attitudes are important, since the parties closest to the workplace are usually the best informed and most capable of resolving the problems arising in it.

The most complex of the bargaining process is internal or intraorganizational bargaining. Within management, such bargaining is usually cloaked in secrecy, and, since it involves relatively few individuals, is difficult to assess. The hierarchic nature of management provides relatively explicit lines of authority, permitting the negotiators to contact a superior quickly and offer counterproposals. The union, in contrast, solicits a wide-ranging assortment of member demands. Although it attempts to gauge the priority of each item before negotiations begin, it must weigh the cost of each concession to the group of workers affected before agreeing to a reformulated package of demands. Some tradeoffs are inevitable. Younger workers, for example, are typically most interested in current wages, while older workers are more concerned with health and pension benefits. Skilled workers often have special needs and often demand specific rules or fringe benefits for themselves. As bargaining units become larger, the union negotiator is faced with a delicate set of tradeoffs, making internal bargaining vital for union cohesion. It should be noted that unexpected management proposals, where the reaction of union members is uncertain, may necessitate time-consuming union meetings, putting even more pressure on negotiators to reach a settlement before agreements expire.

If the bargaining process fails to result in an agreement before the contract expiration date, a strike often ensues, since most unions maintain a "no contract, no work" policy. Strikes and lockouts are not as frequent as is often supposed—fewer than 5 percent of all negotiations end in strikes. In 1976, for example, the 5,600 strikes which began involved only 2.5 million workers, less than 3 percent of all workers.[17] The average duration of strikes is relatively short, only 15.2 days in 1976. The three measures of strikes ("work stoppages" in the statistics)—the total number, the number of workers involved, and days idle (as a percent of total work time)—fluctuate each year, since most labor agreements are for two or three years. In 1974, for example, the lifting of wage-price controls and the expiration of a number of contracts produced over 6,000 strikes involving nearly 2.8 million workers, the most strike-prone year in recent history.

Although strike activity appears to be on the increase in all the industrialized countries, the primary reason for work stoppages—wage disputes—remains unchanged. About half of all strikes result from disagreement over wage increases, a proportion which has remained relatively constant in recent years. The only other single issue prompting significant strike activity was plant administration procedures, reported as the cause of about one fourth of all strikes in 1976. Since World War II, most strikes and strikers have been in nonmanufacturing industries, but this trend is reversed in years of major manufacturing strikes. In 1976, for example, a four-month rubber industry strike and a two-month strike against the Ford Motor Company resulted in far more days lost because of strikes in manufacturing than in nonmanufacturing industries. As manufacturing employment continues declining and collective bargaining in the expanding service and public sectors is established, it appears that strike activity will once again come to center in nonmanufacturing arenas.

Statistics on the distribution and duration of strikes say little about the *causes* of strikes. Although the union acts as the aggressor in ordering a strike, its action may have been prompted by employer intransigence in bargaining. An employer can (and frequently does) prompt a strike by refusing to make concessions. Since even passive nonaction can engender strikes, it is safest to conclude that a strike is only the tangible product of a failure to agree. Culpability for failure to agree is another issue, one which can be ascertained only on a case-by-case basis. Thus, an increase in strike activity is not necessarily indicative of more militant unions; it may merely reflect renewed employer aggressiveness.

The high cost of strikes to both unions and management as well as the general public has stimulated efforts to find alternatives for dispute settlement. The strike remains the primary union weapon in disputes over *interests*, the issues which arise when negotiating an agreement. Nonstrike alternatives are most common in disputes over *rights*, that is, grievances arising from disagreement in interpreting the agreement in force. The most common strike alternative is arbitration of grievances—some 95 percent of all contracts now

---

[17]Strikes exhibit a peculiar seasonality. Most strikes begin in spring and summer, simply because one of the most effective deterrents to strikes and picketing is the discomfort of winter weather. In 1974, for example, two thirds of the 6,074 strikes began between April and September.

provide for the arbitration of grievances, permitting a neutral outsider to make a decision binding on both parties. Although some grievances still result in **wildcat strikes** (those not authorized by the union leadership), especially in mining, most grievances are settled without work or production losses.[18]

Effective strike alternatives in disputes over interests have been more difficult to find. Before a strike or lockout, the parties must report their intentions to an office of the Federal Mediation and Conciliation Service, but the FMCS cannot enjoin the threatened strike or lockout. Mediators do intervene to try to locate areas of agreement, thus promoting voluntary settlement, but their services are utilized only with the consent of both parties. Other strike alternatives, including continuous bargaining (steel), mandatory "cooling-off" periods (where work continues for eighty days after contract expiration), and compulsory arbitration, have not won widespread acclaim. Both unions and management are reluctant to surrender decision-making power to an outsider, and neither side is eager to give up its ultimate economic weapon, the right to cease or offer work. Although collective bargaining has been subjected to new strains and pressures, it remains a resilient institution, so far capable of allowing the private negotiation of agreements without massive disruption.

Theories of Collective Bargaining

Thus far, we have traced the evolution of bargaining structures, the procedures followed by unions and management when negotiating a new agreement, and the bargaining power each side possesses. But what role does collective bargaining play in today's society? Is collective bargaining merely a technique for preserving labor peace or does it serve both narrow economic and broad sociopolitical goals? In this section, we examine some of the salient theories of collective bargaining to indicate both its generality and its limitations.

One of the clearest definitions of both the generality and purposes of collective bargaining was provided by Selig Perlman at the time when basic labor legislation was being enacted in America. In Perlman's view:

> Collective bargaining is not just a means of raising wages and improving conditions of employment. Nor is it merely democratic government in industry. It is above all a technique whereby an inferior social class or group carries on a never slackening pressure for a bigger share in the social sovereignty as well as for more welfare, security, and liberty for its individual members. As such it is not confined to a single arena, the industrial one, where employers and

---

[18]Some unions use grievances to alter the contract while it is in force. When a strong union negotiates a national or regional agreement with a diverse set of employers, as in trucking, the union can engage in "grievance bargaining," using grievances to extract additional benefits from selected employers. For a study of grievance bargaining in the rubber and electrical appliance industries, see J. Kuhn, *Bargaining in Grievance Settlement* (New York: Columbia University Press, 1961).

labor unions meet directly, but manifests itself equally in politics, legislation, court litigation, government administration, religion, education, and propaganda.[19]

Perlman found evidence of collective bargaining in diverse historical circumstances, from the early struggles between town merchants and feudal lords in Europe to the later struggles of journeymen craftsmen against the merchant-capitalists. For Perlman, collective bargaining is a technique for asserting the rights of an emergent class—first merchants, then craftsmen, later industrial workers, and now (presumably) public sector workers. The claims of the emergent class clash with established rights and privileges, as Marx predicted. But Perlman held that collective bargaining between the new class and its established adversary " . . . is pragmatic and concrete instead of idealist and abstract." Instead of displacing established classes, collective bargaining was held to be a limited tool, an instrument useful "to gain equal rights as a class and equal consideration for the members of that [emergent] class with the members of that other [established] class."[20]

The idea that job-centered collective bargaining is the *raison d'etre* of American unionism holds sway to this day. But Perlman's insistence on narrow "business unionism" is being swept aside by an array of both predictable and unpredictable forces. Rising educational levels make the individual worker more articulate in voicing his/her desires and demanding at least limited control over the job. Longer life expectancy and greater affluence lead to demands for expanded pensions and more leisure time instead of mandatory overtime work. Thus, the scope of bargaining expands as a result of the changed attitudes of union members, attitudes produced by underlying demographic, economic, and social trends.

The most significant factor increasing the scope of collective bargaining is the intervention of government in the economy and in the employment relationship. Intervention to assure economic efficiency clashes with union **featherbedding** or "safe manning" (adequate workforces) drives. Government intervention to balance persisting inflationary and unemployment pressures has resulted in a legacy of attempts to constrain the permissible behavior of unions and management. In addition to expecting collective bargaining to result in agreements which are both efficient and compatible with national economic policies, the government considers intervention when failed negotiations threaten inconvenience, as when strikes shut down schools and airlines or halt mail deliveries. Finally, public policy has made individual and minority rights of paramount importance. Intervention to assure internal democratic procedures (within unions) enjoys widespread acceptance, but intervention to assure equal

---

[19]S. Perlman, "The Principle of Collective Bargaining," *The Annals of the American Academy of Political and Social Sciences,* March, 1936, p. 155.

[20]Ibid., p. 156.

or remedial access in employment is often resisted by both unions and management.

The net effect of these changes remains ambiguous. Collective bargaining has proved to be a useful instrument for labor peace, flexible enough to provide industrial self-government in a diverse set of circumstances. The new demands placed on collective bargaining appear disruptive because they often produce incompatibilities, as in requirements for affirmative action which clash with established seniority systems. Before collective bargaining is strained beyond the bounds of its normal elasticity, society may have to make some hard choices about the social goals which deserve highest priority. It may be necessary, for example, to leave seniority intact and redress discrimination through financial inducements to employers and unions if the system of free collective bargaining is to survive.

Collective bargaining affords the individual worker a unique power in modern industrial society. Political democracy affords the worker an equal vote with his supervisor on election day, but organization gives the individual a voice in the economic decisions affecting him daily. Just as society enacts legislation to govern the interrelationships between groups and individuals, so collective bargaining results in a set of workplace rules and procedures. Although legislation could be substituted for the rules established during collective bargaining, such an extension of public intervention dilutes the decision-making power of the parties closest to the workplace—the union and management involved. Collective bargaining, with results and procedures bounded by economics and law, has proven a highly successful device for resolving the inevitable conflict arising in employment. Unless subject to intolerable strain, collective bargaining can continue to serve as the "second" participatory democracy for the organized work force.

Summary

Collective bargaining is a power-based relationship between union(s) and management, each with separate goals and needs. As a power relationship, the union-management interaction is subject to change. Relative power (or the willingness to use power) changes with leadership changes, legal enactments, internal organization threats, or economic changes. The wide variety of factors influencing relative union and management power imparts a dynamism to labor relations, with first one and then the other side possessing the upper hand in bargaining.

Negotiations between unions and management follow an established pattern. The appropriate bargaining unit is given by law and tradition, while the scope of bargaining is primarily determined by relative bargaining power. Most agreements are negotiated by revising an existing agreement in accord with some pattern or master settlement. In "major agreements," covering 1,000 or more workers, teams of negotiators bargain, receiving guidance from the existing agreement, the company's position, union needs, and the overall economic picture.

Negotiations to establish or revise labor agreements settle conflicting union-management *interests*. Since there is no basis for establishing a "just" settlement of these interests, agreement is forced by the ability of each party to impose costs on its adversary for disagreement. Most negotiations are concluded without a work stoppage, and result in a written agreement for a specified period, usually two or three years.

The written agreement sets wages and hours but also establishes *rights,* rights which are given meaning only during the daily workplace interactions between supervisors and individual employees. Disputes over rights result in the filing of grievances, complaints which are resolved in an appeals process whose final arbiter is usually a neutral, outside arbitrator. In addition to rights under the agreement, the worker, unlike a ton of steel, possesses rights in employment provided by law. In the next chapter, we examine these twin bundles of rights, those granted by the agreement and those granted by law.

Bibliography

Chamberlin, N., and J. Kuhn. *Collective Bargaining.* New York: McGraw-Hill, 1965.

   The most thorough treatment available of the evolution, structure, and process of collective bargaining.

Flanders, A., ed. *Collective Bargaining.* New York: Penguin, 1969.

   A useful collection of essays by the leading specialists.

Labor Law and Contract Administration

7

In the world of labor, the terms "fair," "just cause," "reasonable," "in good faith," and "concerted activity" recur frequently. The words themselves are ambiguous—a "fair wage" in the employer's eyes may be quite different than a worker's conception of a "fair wage." These terms must be given meaning in the context of concrete situations—was an employee who refused to work in winter when the plant was without heat fired for "just cause"? Most of the ambiguity is resolved between union and employer, but both parties are guided by a set of established labor principles and their interpretations. In this chapter, we explore the labor laws which serve to guide the conduct of labor relations and examine one type of conduct in some detail: the handling of grievances arising from the administration of a collective bargaining agreement.

Both public and private laws and policies provide a framework for labor relations which channels and minimizes industrial strife while assuring equitable treatment to individuals, employers, and unions. The public framework (the labor relations laws) and the private framework (grievance mechanisms and arbitration) recognize the inevitability of interest conflicts and contract disputes. But mutual interdependence in production and employment gives all parties incentives to anticipate conflict and channel it in directions which cause minimal production and wage losses. The first part of this chapter explores the public framework for controlling and guiding the organizing and negotiating actions of the parties, and the second part examines the procedures which unions and employers have developed to settle disputes during the life of the labor contract, the grievance and arbitration mechanism.

When negotiating an agreement, the bargaining parties' strategies and tactics are guided by economic and organizational concerns. But not all strategies and tactics mandated by economic or organizational factors are lawful. If either party engages in actions which violate labor laws, it loses its protections under the National Labor Relations Act and may be subject to suit for remedy. Thus, the law acts as an important guide and restraint on the behavior of bargaining adversaries.

Labor laws are of two distinct types. Labor relations law, whose evolution was traced in Chapter 2, defines the rights and duties of individuals, unions, and employers in the course of organizing workers and negotiating agreements covering hours, wages, and other terms of employment. But another important set of labor laws exists—those protecting individual workers in case of on-the-job injury, unemployment, or old age. These protective labor laws tend to erect *minimum* levels of health, safety, and old age protection, minimums which a union can supplement when bargaining.

Protective labor laws in America provide fewer benefits to injured, unemployed, or retired workers than do their more comprehensive counterparts in Europe. To cushion the abrupt change in economic status which accompanies injury, unemployment, and retirement in America (as well as to minimize benefit variation across states), American unions are forced to negotiate agreements covering matters often left to government in other countries, helping to explain the complexity of American labor agreements. Although American social policy is expanding to embrace more workers and provide increased benefits, it remains among the least generous in industrialized nations.

Protective labor laws affect bargaining strategies by providing government-mandated minimum standards from which negotiations can begin. But labor law does more than merely erect floors for bargaining positions—it directly impinges on the use of economic power and hence bargaining power. For example, many establishments rely on trucks to transport supplies and finished products. If production workers strike but drivers are permitted to honor their picket lines, the bargaining power of the striking production workers is increased. Although the courts have declared that no specific interpretation of a labor law should attempt to balance the economic power of bargaining adversaries, it is clear that specific legal interpretations can exert significant influence on relative bargaining power.

Unions and managements found the public framework of control inadequate for the myriad of minor conflicts which arise in the process of production and supervision, prompting the erection of a system of "industrial self-government." In this system, the collective bargaining agreement serves as the "written constitution" and the grievance and arbitration mechanism as the judiciary. Thus, a parallel system of private control evolved to complement the established public control over labor relations. As we survey the salient labor laws and grievance procedures, it is important to remember that written legal and arbitration decisions cover only the egregious cases; one would get a very biased picture of day-to-day labor relations by reading only the results of those cases which prompted court or arbitration review.

The Law of Collective Bargaining

One of the purposes of the Wagner Act was to increase employee bargaining power to permit higher wages, wages whose spending would generate increased demand for goods and services and help fuel recovery from the Depression. Since 1935, labor legislation has avoided reference to its economic consequences—amendments in 1947 and 1959 confine their concern to labor peace and the rights of employers, employees, and unions. Although the courts have repeatedly adduced the principle that interpretations of labor law "should not attempt to balance the economic power of the parties," numerous NLRB and court decisions have had significant impacts on the relative strengths of unions and employers. In this section, the salient aspects of contemporary labor law are reviewed.

In the absence of a union, the employer may unilaterally establish hours, wages, and working conditions. Each individual may accept the terms offered by an employer or seek work elsewhere. A nonunion employer is free to change wages and working conditions (provided he does not violate a protective labor law such as the minimum wage or safety standards), but the employees are also free to protest, individually or en masse. Section 7 of the NLRA protects employee "concerted activities" with or without a union, and the courts have held that even a protest by one individual over conditions affecting at least one other person is a protected activity. In a now-famous legal decision, seven nonunion machinists who walked out to protest a lack of heat in the plant were protected from discharge. The court held that, in the absence of a union, no *specific* demand (e.g., for a temperature of 72°F) is necessary before nonunion workers engage in a protected concerted activity, since nonunion workers have no bargaining representatives through which complaints could be filtered.[1]

The presence of a union alters the relatively simple relationship between employer and employee. Now three "bundles of rights" are involved—the rights of employers, acting alone or in multiemployer groups; the rights of unions; and the rights of employees, vis-á-vis both employers and their unions. Four types of legal issues impinge directly on the collective bargaining process:

1. The right of employees to unfettered organization
2. The determination of bargaining units and bargaining representatives
3. The duty to bargain "in good faith"
4. The role of strikes, pickets, and lockouts

The complexity of strike and lockout issues leads to their separate consideration in a later section. Before turning to specific legal issues, we review the legal mechanisms through which complaints pass.

The web of rule governing labor relations has been established over time by both the courts and administrative agencies. The National Labor Relations Board (NLRB) is the primary interpreter of labor law. An administrative agency established under the NLRA in 1935, the NLRB consists of five members, appointed by the President for five-year terms. The NLRB is assisted by a general counsel, who has final authority over the issuance of unfair labor prac-

---

[1]*NLRB* v. *Washington Aluminum Company*, 370 U.S. 9, 82 Supreme Court 1099 (1962).

tice complaints, investigations, and the NLRB's various regional offices, where legal issues first arise.

The NLRB hears two types of cases, those claiming that unfair labor practices have been committed and those emanating from representation elections. In the unfair labor practice cases, the NLRB machinery is silent until a charge is filed (theoretically, *anyone* could file a charge, although most charges are filed by unions and employers). An NLRB regional office schedules a hearing on the complaint before an administrative law judge, who issues an "intermediate report." In most instances, the report terminates the matter, but either party may appeal to the NLRB within twenty days. On appeal to the NLRB, the administrative law judge's report may be upheld, rejected, or modified. Most reports are upheld, and result in NLRB **cease-and-desist orders** requiring the employer or union to abstain from certain actions and including provisions for remedy and dissemination of the NLRB's order among, for example, the affected employees.

The authority of the NLRB ends with its cease-and-desist orders. But the law is sprinkled with the words "reasonable," "discriminate," "interfere with," "good faith," and so on. Since these words are subject to interpretation, the law provides for appeal of NLRB decisions to the courts. The aggrieved party may appeal an NLRB decision to one of the eleven U.S. courts of appeal. The court of appeals can enforce the NLRB decision by issuing a contempt of court ruling, holding union or corporate leaders personally responsible for failing to carry out NLRB orders. Alternatively, the court of appeals may reverse the NLRB decision or order the case returned until further evidence is obtained. Dissatisfaction in the court of appeals can prompt a Supreme Court review, although the Supreme Court declines to review most cases appealed to it. Throughout the appeal process, NLRB findings on the *facts* in the dispute are usually accepted—the courts rule only on questions of law.

Now that the complexity of appellate procedure is clear, let's return to specific legal disputes under labor law. Before collective bargaining can occur, a bargaining unit must be established and bargaining representatives selected. In general, individuals are permitted "free choice" in selecting between unions or electing a nonunion option. Both unions and employers are expected to refrain from inappropriate electioneering tactics; the company, for example, cannot promise benefits or threaten retribution contingent on the results of a union election.[2] It should be remembered that actions and speeches normally pro-

---

[2]A perennial issue is the lawfulness of employer threats to "go out of business" if the union wins an election. In such situations, two rights conflict, the right of free and unrestrained organization and the right of an employer to go out of business. In such situations, the Supreme Court has held "that when an employer closes his entire business, even if the liquidation is motivated by vindictiveness toward the union, such action is not an unfair labor practice." *Textile Workers Union* v. *Darlington Manufacturing Company* and *NLRB* v. *Darlington Manufacturing Company* 380, U.S. 263 (1965). Another issue, the veracity of statements made during an organizing campaign, has evolved from initial attempts by the NLRB to rule on the "truthfulness" of campaign statements to a recognition that employees are sophisticated enough to sort out truth and propaganda in organizational campaigns.

tected by First Amendment "free speech" rights are not necessarily allowed during union organizing campaigns.

Unions are selected as bargaining representatives in several ways. If both union and employer agree on the scope of the bargaining unit (which employees are to be included) and that the union is desired by a majority of the employees in the bargaining unit, the employer can simply recognize the union as bargaining representative. If employee sentiments are unclear or if the employer contests the union's claim, an election is held. The election decides a single issue—does the union (or which union, if several unions are competing) represent a majority of eligible employees who voted?

The NLRB (and its regional offices) have complete control over election procedures. After the union demonstrates employee support, usually by obtaining signed and dated "authorization cards" from 30 percent of the relevant workers, the NLRB (or its agent) determines who is eligible to vote, what choices appear on the ballot, the date of the election, and the rules and procedures governing balloting. The NLRB or its agent issues a "direction of election" and provides poll watchers. The union is certified if it receives a majority vote among all valid votes cast; that is, it needs only a majority among those voting, not a majority among all workers.

Although the election procedure appears straightforward, it produces a variety of real-life issues. To take a simple example, determining who is eligible to vote, it would be simple if those working were those voting. Even such a simple rule must confront the situation of employees on sick leave or vacation or those employees temporarily laid off. The NLRB has ruled that those workers temporarily absent may vote if they appear at the polling place on the day of the election, making no provision for absentee ballots. Employees on strike present another problem. Those on strike for economic reasons, even if replaced by another worker (who may also vote), are eligible to vote up to twelve months after the strike began. Workers striking to protest an employer's unfair labor practice can vote as long as the strike continues, but their replacements cannot. Thus, even an issue as simple as eligibility for voting becomes complex because of the variety of situations found in the working world.

Unions are certified as representatives of workers in "bargaining units." What constitutes an "appropriate bargaining unit"? The NLRB is given considerable discretion in determining whether "the unit appropriate for collective bargaining shall be the employer unit, craft unit, plant unit, or subdivision thereof." Bargaining power is directly affected by bargaining unit determination, with unions typically favoring more inclusive units to increase bargaining power while employers argue that multiple "communities of interest" exist, requiring multiple bargaining units. Since the Taft-Hartley Act (1947), employees have the right to refrain from union activities, and one result has been to require that professional and nonprofessional workers be in separate bargaining units unless a majority of the professionals agree to be part of the overall unit.

Most bargaining unit determinations are made on the basis of past bargaining history, the type of industry, and the desires of employees. The most provocative issue involves craft workers—should skilled workers be allowed to establish separate bargaining units? In the days of competition between the AFL and the CIO, the CIO favored plantwide unionism to maximize the bargaining power of unskilled employees. The AFL, on the other hand, encouraged "craft severance," since its unions organized workers on the basis of skill. The NLRB has vacillated, first ruling that the issue of separate craft units should be decided in plantwide elections, where unskilled employees constitute a majority, and subsequently ruling that a craft unit was justified if the workers truly represented a craft and the craft workers had maintained a separate identity over time. The issue remains alive today. Craft workers in the automobile industry, for example, have been pressing for separate bargaining representation, although the NLRB has refused to permit craft severance in this instance.

Once appropriate bargaining units are determined and bargaining representatives selected, the union and employer are required to bargain over "wages, hours, and other terms and conditions of employment." The certified union is the *exclusive* bargaining agent for unit employees, and both the union and the employer are required to bargain in good faith with the union over wages and working conditions. This "good-faith" requirement mandates that the parties must: (1) meet at reasonable times, (2) confer to reach agreement, (3) draw up a written contract *if* agreement is reached, and (4) give a sixty-day notice to terminate or modify an existing agreement. Good-faith bargaining does *not* require agreement—it only obligates the parties to propose "honestly" and make counterproposals. Both the NLRB and the courts infer good-faith behavior from the actions of the parties, not from the extent of their agreement or disagreement.

Bargaining topics fall in three categories. *Mandatory* subjects of bargaining are "wages, hours, and other terms and conditions of employment." Some bargaining subjects are *prohibited,* including union demands which force an employer to discriminate unlawfully against an employee or to demand concessions which contravene other federal statutes, such as demands for wage increases in time of wage-price freezes. Union demands for the closed shop (requiring union membership before hire) or "hot cargo" clauses, which do not permit the employer to deal with certain third parties, were prohibited by the Taft-Hartley Act in 1947 and the Landrum-Griffin Act in 1959.

The ambiguity of "other terms of employment" has produced a class of bargaining subjects which are neither mandatory nor prohibited. These permissible bargaining subjects may be raised by either party, but the other party is free to ignore them. No major economic weapon may be utilized to force concessions on permissible bargaining topics—strikes and lockouts are reserved for disagreement on mandatory bargaining issues. An example of a permissible but not mandatory bargaining subject is the level of benefits to be provided already retired workers.[3] Other examples include employee contributions to an industry promotion fund and a company demand that individual employees sign their

---

[3]See *Allied Chemical Workers Local 1* v. *Pittsburgh Plate Glass Company,* 404, U.S. 157 (1971).

grievance petitions. Since each new permissible subject over which the union can induce bargaining further limits managerial discretion, it is the union which usually acts to increase the number of bargaining subjects.

A recurring issue before the NLRB is the legality of employer "final offer" negotiations. This bargaining tactic, sometimes termed "Boulwarism" after the General Electric vice president who initiated it, has the company anticipating union demands and making a "fair and firm" offer, at the initial bargaining session, subject to change only if new information is presented during negotiations. In final offer situations, the employer often communicates directly with the workers to secure support for its contract proposal, bypassing the union.

The unions vigorously attacked this "final offer" approach to collective bargaining as a breach of the good faith duty to bargain. If the employer's right to present a "final offer" were upheld, then the union was reduced to merely a grievance advocate, losing any meaningful role in the negotiation of new contracts. But the NLRB declared final offer bargaining an unfair labor practice, designed to "disparage the union . . . rather than to satisfy the true standards and good faith collective bargaining required by the statute."[4] Although the law cannot force either party to make specific concessions, it prohibits either party from presenting a set of bargaining proposals and announcing that terms are immutable in the course of bargaining.

Dispute Settlement

If the bargaining parties fail to reach an agreement, each side deploys the means at its disposal to force concessions and agreement on its own terms. The primary economic weapons to force concessions are the union's **strike** and **picketing,** sometimes countered by the employer's **lockout,** in which employees are prevented from working at their jobs. In most instances, the bargaining parties are able to reach agreement without resort to strikes and lockouts. In 1976, for example, the 5,600 strikes which occurred involved less than 3 percent of the labor force.[5] Strikes and lockouts are the exception rather than the rule in collective bargaining; typically, over 95 percent of all contracts are negotiated without resort to work stoppages.

Labor law is complex because it regulates many actions which would be entirely legal if pursued individually but fall under legal purview when engaged in collectively. Any individual worker is free to cease work when desired, just

---

[4]*General Electric Company,* 150, NLRB 192 (1965).

[5]The number of strikes varies with the number of expiring contracts in any year and the propensity of unions and management to strike or "take a strike" rather than concede. The number of strikes rose from about 3,300 annually in the early 1960s to 5,700 per year in 1969–1970. The number of strikes decreased during the era of wage-price controls (1971–1973) but reached a postwar peak of 6,000 in 1974.

as any customer may disparage those goods and services he or she dislikes. But the *collective* exercise of the right to stop working or picketing to discourage the purchase of certain goods and services becomes "concerted action" under the National Labor Relations Act. Not all "concerted activities for the purpose of collective bargaining or other mutual aid or protection" are legal, requiring an examination of permissible union and employer tactics to force concessions.

The right to strike, for workers collectively to withhold their labor power, is the basic source of union power. Employers generate profits (and workers obtain wages) only when production occurs; hence, the cessation of work imposes costs on both employers and striking workers. To minimize losses, the employer attempts to continue production and sales, while the striking workers seek to increase pressure on the employer by picketing and boycotting to discourage the production and sale of goods and services.

The right to strike is a limited right. In 1965, the Supreme Court asserted that "the right to strike as commonly understood is the right to cease work — nothing more."[6] The law recognizes two types of strikes, those intended to put economic pressure on an employer when negotiating a contract (i.e., economic strikes), and strikes called to protest employer actions which violate the National Labor Relations Act, so-called **unfair labor practice strikes.** Under the law, striker rights to reinstatement and back pay vary with the type of strike.

Economic strikes, during which workers cease work to force employer concessions in contract negotiations, afford the striking worker the least protection. When an economic striker ceases work, the employer may legally hire permanent replacements to operate his business. Once a permanent replacement is hired, the striker loses any automatic right to reemployment, although he or she remains an employee of the struck employer for twelve months or until the striker finds "substantially equivalent employment" elsewhere. If, for example, a work force of one hundred goes on strike and the employer hires fifty permanent replacements before agreement is reached, the employer is only required to take fifty of the strikers back, although they must be rehired in a nondiscriminatory fashion (usually on the basis of ability to do the job and seniority).[7]

If an employer can replace economic strikers permanently, it could be assumed that economic strikes would be rare because of the threat of job loss to individual workers. Strikes are costly — the worker loses wages, the union must pay strike benefits, and other producers can encroach on the struck employer's markets. But few employers attempt to replace strikers permanently, primarily because an employer cannot hire enough skilled workers to operate his plant on a moment's notice. Even if replacements were available, most employers re-

---

[6]*American Shipbuilding Company* v. *NLRB*, 380, U.S. 300 (1965).

[7]If the employer, in rehiring strikers, discriminates against union activists, for example, an unfair labor practice is committed, and the employer can be required to take back the strikers even if permanent replacements have been hired. *NLRB* v. *McKay Radio and Telegraph Company*, 304, U.S. 333 (1938).

frain from operation during a strike because of the violence engendered by hiring scabs. The employer *could* systematically begin replacing strikers, and some employers do, but most employers realize that they must eventually come to terms with the union, causing them to refrain from actions which would unduly jeopardize eventual agreement.

Strikes impose costs on both participating workers and employers and on workers and employers not directly involved in the dispute. An auto strike may, for example, lead to layoffs and losses for workers and employers making auto parts or tires, just as a longshore strike can lead to unemployment among truck drivers as well as inconveniencing customers of goods transported by ship. In most instances, these costs to other workers, employers, and the public at large are accepted as a reasonable price for industrial self-regulation. But some strikes impose such widespread costs that they are considered a threat to "national health and safety," and are constrained by law.

A national emergency dispute is defined in the Taft-Hartley Act (1947) as "an actual or threatened strike or lockout which, if permitted to occur or continue, will (in the opinion of the President) constitute a threat to the national health or safety." If the President determines a strike to be precipitating a national emergency, he is empowered to order a board of inquiry to investigate the facts of the dispute, order the strikers back to work for eighty days (the "cooling-off" period), and have the NLRB conduct a union membership vote on the employer's final offer. If the dispute remains unsettled after eighty days, the strike may be resumed, and the President may recommend that Congress enact a legislative remedy. Separate emergency dispute settlement procedures exist for railroad and airline disputes.

Between 1949 and 1972, the national emergency dispute provisions of the Taft-Hartley Act were invoked twenty-nine times. In nine of the interventions, all in longshoring disputes, the strikes were resumed after the eighty-day work injunction expired. Because national emergency dispute procedures do not result in a "final" settlement, they have been criticized for being an unwarranted and ineffective infringement in the exercise of "free" collective bargaining. Other criticisms, including the ambiguity of the term "national health and safety," have prompted some to argue that national emergency procedures should be abolished, but economic interdependency and the real external crises imposed by (some) strikes lends support for the maintenance of some form of emergency intervention.

Economic strikes expose the striker to the risk of permanent replacement, but unfair labor practice strikes do not. Under Section 7 of the NLRA, employees have the right to engage in "concerted activities," including concerted work stoppages, to further collective bargaining aims or to provide "mutual aid or protection." Section 8(a) of the NLRA makes it unlawful for an employer "to interfere with, restrain, or coerce employees in the exercise of the rights guaranteed in Section 7." Thus, general employer interference or specific actions, including employer domination of a labor organization, discrimination against workers to discourage unionization, or failure to bargain with designated employee representatives, constitute employer unfair labor practices. If employees call an unfair labor practice strike to protest these employer actions, they enjoy the right of reinstatement if they make an unconditional application for reemployment. In addition to enjoying reemployment rights, unfair labor practice strikers are entitled to collect back pay from the time of the employer's refusal to reinstate them.

The problem with unfair labor practices is that a determination of the lawfulness of employer actions is made only *after* it occurs. Thus, if workers *think* that an employer has committed an unfair labor practice and strike, but the NLRB determines that the employer's actions were lawful, the strikers can be summarily discharged and the union held liable for damages, if the agreement contained a no-strike clause. The law permits unfair labor practice strikes despite no-strike clauses, but the fact that an "objective" determination of the lawfulness of the employer's action is made only after the strike occurs subjects the striking worker to considerable risk unless the employer's action clearly violates labor law. Most unfair labor practice strikes are called only after rather blatant employer actions, since workers are aware of the risks they assume in protest.

In addition to striking, the union usually seeks to bolster its position by picketing to inform other workers and potential customers that a labor dispute is in progress. Picketing is sometimes termed "coercive communication," since "the object of all picketing at all times is to influence third persons to withhold their business or services from the struck employer."[8] Picketing is one of the most controversial issues in labor law, since the First Amendment guarantees individuals certain rights of "free speech." Picketing presents a classic clash of fundamental rights. Employers have the right to operate a business as they see fit (subject to law), and individuals have the right to spend their money in any business they choose. The picketing problem arises when one group of individuals seeks to enlist the support of others to exert greater pressure on an employer or a particular business establishment. Those picketing are seeking support from third-party neutrals, and the legal issue becomes a problem of separating the rights of free speech and communication from both business and individual rights. The overriding objectives remain the "free flow of commerce" and labor peace, forcing the courts to search for an "accommodation between the two [rights . . .] with as little destruction of one as is consistent with the maintenance of the other."[9]

---

[8]*Teamsters Local 807* (Schultz Refrigerated Service, Inc.) 87 NLRB 502.

[9]*NLRB* v. *Babcock and Wilcox Company*, 351, U.S. 105 (1956). In this case, the Supreme Court was balancing another set of conflicting rights, the organizational rights of employees and the property rights of the Babcock and Wilcox Company. The company's plant, located within a fenced enclosure one mile from the community, had limited gate access. The Supreme Court voided the NLRB's finding that the parking lot and walkways leading to the plant were the only "safe and practicable" places for distributing union literature, holding that nonemployee (outside) organizers could have used other means to communicate with employees and that the company had a long-standing policy of prohibiting *all* solicitation and literature distribution on company property. Normally, private property rights yield to organizational rights only if company property is the only "safe and practicable place" to distribute union literature and solicit union authorization signatures.

The movement from direct strike or picket activity against the employer with whom a dispute actually exists (the *primary* employer) to actions against noninvolved parties opens a complex array of legal issues. If a union has a dispute with an employer and seeks to put pressure on that employer by appealing to the workers of other *(secondary)* employers, the union is engaging in secondary or indirect activities. The law governing lawful secondary activities is the most complex in traditional labor relations law. In general, a union may not induce employees of a "truly neutral" secondary employer to cease performing their duties to pressure the secondary employer into halting all transactions with the primary employer, that is, the employer with whom the union has a dispute. If a union of shoemakers had a dispute with a shoe manufacturing company and succeeded in getting shoe salesmen to cease work by picketing shoe stores (a **secondary boycott**), it would be the shoemakers' union which would be charged with having committed an unfair labor practice.

The law governing secondary activities regulates a variety of situations. The strike, confined to the workers and employer directly involved, concentrates its costs on the parties to the dispute. As soon as outside support is enlisted, "neutrals" get involved. Since the union is usually first to seek third party support, Section 8(b)(4) of the NLRA is directed toward lawful and unlawful secondary activities of unions. In general, secondary union activities which violate *both* parts of a double "unlawfulness" test are prohibited, subjecting the union to damage liability. Activities will be found to be unlawful if: (1) the union's objective is unlawful (e.g., the union attempts to induce the employees of a secondary employer to cease work), *and* (2) the means used by the union to achieve its objectives are unlawful (e.g., violent or coercive picketing). Only if *both* of the unlawfulness tests are fulfilled is the union liable for punishment under the NLRA.

Contract Administration: Grievance Procedures and Arbitration

Successful negotiations between the union and an employer result in a written collective bargaining agreement. But what does the agreement "really mean"? If a worker can be fired only "for cause," is tardiness sufficient cause for discharge? What if the company decides that all workers shall wear uniforms after the agreement has been signed? Since the topic is not mentioned in the agreement, must employee Jones wear a uniform against his will? The signed agreement is given life only through its application to the day-to-day disputes which arise in the workplace. Since these disputes arise continually, a grievance mechanism has been established to resolve such workplace disputes on a case-by-case basis, permitting work to continue but assuring "fair treatment" to both parties.

The establishment of the **grievance procedure** to handle recurring workplace disputes has been called the "core of the collective bargaining agreement.'' Although the agreement can specify uniform wages and hours, employment conditions are extremely varied, forcing the bargainers to rely on more general language to cover working conditions. As specific situations arise, the agreement's general language must be interpreted and applied to particular problems. This interplay between union and management in settling disputes between an individual or individuals and a supervisor erects a system of industrial jurisprudence, with the union acting as advocate for the aggrieved work or work group while the employer backs his supervisor. Both sides appeal according to a defined set of rules and procedures. The substitution of complaint and appeal helps prevent arbitrary actions and eliminates much of the need for wildcat strikes and other disorders frequently used by workers to draw attention to a particular problem.

Before the establishment of grievance procedures, collective bargaining, with its omnipresent threat of strikes, pickets, and lockouts, was invoked each time a dispute arose, such as when a (group of) worker(s) felt the employer was not ''living up to the agreement'' or a situation arose which was not mentioned by the agreement. Since these disputes arose almost daily, labor relations were unstable, with neither side sure of the outcome because of fluctuations in bargaining power. In the early decades of the twentieth century, unions in the building trades, the coal fields, and textile and apparel manufacturing began employing roving union agents to police employer conformance with agreements. Despite the increased certainty of production and employment introduced by continuing compliance with the agreement, employers were reluctant to accept grievance procedures, fearing that they surrendered too many inherent management rights to unions. Grievance procedures became common during World War II, when the National War Labor Board encouraged their inclusion in labor contracts.

The usefulness of grievance procedures is evidenced by their widespread acceptance in collective bargaining agreements. In 1974, only 16 (1 percent) of the 1,550 major agreements in force contained no reference to grievance or arbitration procedures. Most agreements provide for procedures to assure due process in workplace disputes which culminate in arbitration, a decision binding on both parties. In 1974, over 97 percent of all major agreements provided for final arbitration (usually by an outside neutral) of any disputes not settled in the meetings between union and management. The acceptance of grievance and arbitration procedures, advocated by unions in the 1930s and 1940s when employers were resisting ''encroachment'' of management rights in personnel matters, does much to explain the labor peace which normally prevails while agreements are in force.

The acceptance of grievance procedures in American labor relations incorporated two principles of contemporary labor relations. The establishment of a grievance mechanism was evidence that both parties *expected* disputes to arise, that is, that both parties recognized the continuing nature of the union-management conflict of interest. But the inclusion of grievance mechanisms also demonstrated the parties' joint recognition that a procedure which allows work to continue while disputes are settled is mutually advantageous, since the workers secure a continuing income and the employer can maintain production. The substitution of due process for bargaining power during the life of a labor agreement has been heralded as one of the major advances in labor relations in this century.

Although grievance procedures vary across industries, every grievance system must address three issues: (1) What is a grievance? (2) What rules and procedures must be followed when pressing grievances? and (3) Is arbitration the final step in the grievance procedure? The grievance and arbitration system constitutes a type of *private* industrial jurisprudence; the courts intervene only to decide if grievances can be pressed, not to decide the merits of the grievance or rule on the fairness of the arbitrator's award. The alternative to (private) arbitration of contract disputes would be individual suits for breach of contract. The increased cost, delay, and technicalities involved with court procedures make arbitration both socially and privately desirable. In reaching a decision, the arbitrator is bound by the contract; his purpose is to interpret the contract in light of the specific incident in dispute.

Since grievances are disputes over "rights" established in the collective bargaining agreement, a grievance usually emanates from a specific incident. The first issue in grievance procedures, then, is the definition of a grievance—are all disputes between an individual (represented by the union) and the employer open to grievance resolution, or only those which result from a disagreement over interpreting the language of the agreement? Does the grievance procedure allow employer complaints about union activities or not? Before the grievance mechanism can be invoked, it must be determined whether a particular incident is covered by the grievance procedure specified in the agreement.

Since labor law is meant to minimize "industrial strife," the courts have been willing to force virtually *all* workplace disputes through the grievance procedure, provided the union and employer have established such a system in the agreement. In one of a famous trilogy of cases involving the United Steelworkers of America, the Supreme Court declared that "the function of the court is very limited when the parties have agreed to submit all questions of contract interpretation to the arbitrator . . . the courts therefore have no business weighing the merits of the grievance . . . [because] the processing of even frivolous claims may have therapeutic values."[10] Thus, virtually *any* grievance filed by union and employer must be put to an arbitrator, including the "arbitratability" of the grievance itself. Since the courts do not review the merits of individual grievances or the reasonableness of the arbitrator's decision, the arbitrator is given considerable power to interpret labor contracts. The arbitrator's discretion is constrained, however, because he must be selected by *both* parties.

The establishment of a grievance procedure invites arbitration over virtu-

---

[10]*United Steelworkers of America* v. *American Manufacturing Company*, 363, U.S. 564 (1960).

ally any workplace dispute.[11] But grievance procedures vary across industries. In the construction industry, the limited duration of employment at each worksite requires quick resolution of disputes. Most construction agreements vest the union's grievance power in a business agent, who patrols the various worksites to ensure that contract terms are met and to solicit union members' complaints. The nature of construction employment often requires on-the-spot adjudication of the complaint. If employer-union agreement cannot be reached, work often ceases. As noted, the ability of the construction union's business agent to halt virtually any project at a moment's notice invests a great deal of power in a single person, sometimes inviting abuse as the contractor strikes a deal with the business agent to continue work.

In most industries, employment is more structured and stable, permitting a well-defined appellate procedure to process the grievance while work continues. The individual worker or workers initially confront their supervisor, with or without the union shop steward. The first level of appeal is an informal meeting between the shop steward (or "grievance man") and a supervisor. Most grievances are quickly resolved in informal discussion between shop steward and supervisor. If they fail to reach agreement, each side writes out its version of events and appeals to the union's shop committee or the plant superintendent. If agreement cannot be reached, the union often enlists the assistance of a national union representative and the personnel director of the company. Since the dispute may be resolved at any stage in the appeals process, only a small fraction of the grievances voiced ever go to arbitration.

The grievance procedure has the structure of a pyramid. Most of the grievances filed by workers are rejected by management, yet most managements are willing to go through the grievance mechanism because the venting of a grievance provides the aggrieved worker a hearing, improving worker morale (grievances can also pinpoint management problems). At the base of the pyramid, most grievances are resolved quickly and informally; since nothing is written, the result becomes only "shopfloor practice." Formality and cost increase as grievances are appealed until, at the level of outside arbitration, written opinions (which may serve as precedent in future disputes) are issued. Since delays and costs (to both parties) increase with appeals,[12] both unions

---

[11]It is important to distinguish the arbitration of rights from arbitration of interests. Interest arbitration seeks to determine what is "fair" or "just," in short, to determine what contract rights *ought to be*. Grievance arbitration, in contrast, merely provides for an extension of particular negotiations (those over the meaning of the contract) and voluntarily vests limited powers in the hands of an outsider, the arbitrator.

[12]Arbitration is both costly and time consuming, discouraging both union and management from pressing truly frivolous grievances. In the early 1960s, Robben Fleming found that an average one-day hearing cost the union $640 and the company $1,025 in fee payments to lawyers and the arbitrator alone. The average time lag between the selection of an arbitration and the issuance of a decision was about four months. See *The Labor Arbitration Process* (Urbana, Ill: University of Illinois Press, 1965), pp. 50–59. It should be noted that both parties may want to avoid arbitration in order to avoid a written precedent on a particular type of grievance.

and management are usually quick to settle the dispute at the lowest possible level.

A collective bargaining agreement is negotiated between a union and an employer or employers, making grievances which arise the property of the union, not the individual worker. The individual (or group) which is aggrieved in a particular incident initiates the grievance process, but the union decides whether to "push" the grievance through the appeal stages or let it drop. No individual employee "has an absolute right to have his grievance taken to arbitration,"[13] but the union is required to represent fairly all those in the bargaining unit, whether they are members of the union or not. If the individual feels that the employer has breached the collective bargaining agreement and the union refuses to press the grievance, the individual can sue both the employer and the union.

The arbitration of grievances is "voluntary" in the sense that union and management agree to abide by the arbitrator's decision rather than resort to strikes or lockouts. Most agreements provide for the selection of an arbitrator each time an unresolved dispute exists, and specify only the mode of selecting an arbitrator rather than a particular individual (e.g., the American Arbitration Association or the Federal Mediation and Conciliation Service may be empowered to name the arbitrator or provide a list of names). In most instances, a single arbitrator decides a dispute, but some agreements call for each side to appoint one or two members to an arbitration board and the appointees to agree on a neutral chairman or "umpire." When the agreement covers thousands of workers, an arbitrator may be retained on a full-time basis, for example, in the auto industry to settle disputes between the UAW and Ford, or between the USW and the U.S. Steel Corporation. In all instances, the arbitrator is constrained by the agreement—he (there are very few female arbitrators) may not add to or subtract from the terms of the agreement.

Most grievances are filed to protest employer disciplinary or discharge actions. If a worker appears for work while intoxicated, and the employer fires him or her, the arbitrator must decide if the firing was for "just cause." In making a decision, the arbitrator looks to the circumstances of the incident (was the individual disorderly?) past practices (is discharge for drunkenness a plant rule?), and policies in other industries. The existence of an arbitration clause in collective bargaining agreements forces management to take a more legalistic approach to discipline, since a management personnel decision may be reviewed by an outside arbitrator. Although discharge and discipline still predominate among grievances, the increased complexity of collective bargaining agreements has resulted in more disputes over health and welfare provisions, other supplementary benefits, and job transfers. The complexity of such contract provisions has forced the local union to increase its reliance on specialist national union representatives when pressing grievances in these areas.

---

[13]*Vaca* v. *Sipes*, 386 U.S. 171 (1967).

Most grievances involve an individual or a small group of workers, that is, a subset or fraction of the labor force. After an agreement is signed, some subgroups who have additional bargaining power can extract additional concessions with *fractional bargaining,*[14] or bargaining through the grievance mechanism. Although discouraged by the union (because of intraunion conflicts and jealousies) as well as the employer (because of the additional concessions necessary), fractional bargaining does occur in such fields as trucking and in some industrial plants. In an era of national or centralized agreements, fractional bargaining can sometimes allow the flexibility denied by uniform national standards.

Summary

Labor relations laws erect a framework for public control of union-management interaction. The nation's basic labor law, enacted in the National Labor Relations Act (1935), provides workers the right to select bargaining representatives and engage in collective bargaining in as "neutral" an environment as possible; that is, the employer may not use his economic power to influence worker preferences. To ensure employer neutrality, the NLRA enumerates several types of employer unfair (unlawful) labor practices. In 1947 and again in 1959, a list of union unfair labor practices, which could be committed against either employers or union members, was added.

The legal regulation of labor relations governs four areas of worker-union-management interaction. Employees have the right to organization without employer interference, the NLRB and the parties jointly determine what bargaining units are appropriate, and the NLRB (and the courts) investigate charges that unions or employers failed to bargain "in good faith" or engaged in prohibited strike, picket, or lockout activities.

In addition to the public labor relations framework, unions and management have erected a private system of industrial jurisprudence, the grievance mechanism. Grievances are usually filed by workers who feel the employer has done something in violation of the agreement. The establishment of grievance mechanisms, usually culminating in arbitration by a mutually agreeable "neutral," has done much to minimize industrial strife during the life of a labor contract.

Grievances charge that (usually individual employee) "rights" granted by the contract have been violated. The arbitrator, when deciding on the merits of the grievance, is constrained to the language and inferences which can be drawn from the contract in force. Most grievances are quickly settled through informal consultation between the individual, the shop steward, and the supervisor, but the appeals process assures that the grievance will get a "fair hearing" even if production continues.

---

[14]See J. Kuhn, *Bargaining in Grievance Settlement* (New York: Columbia University Press, 1961).

Bibliography

Smith, R., et al. *Collective Bargaining and Labor Arbitration.* New York: Bobbs-Merrill, 1970.
A comprehensive source of cases and information on negotiation, the scope of bargaining, and the arbitration of disputes.

————. *Labor Relations Law: Cases and Materials.* New York: Bobbs-Merrill, 1974.
One of the many case books on labor law. A supplement which updates case material is issued periodically.

Public Sector Unionism

8

The first labor unions were defensive reactions to the disruptions initiated by private entrepreneurs. As long as private interests were the immediate cause of disruption as well as the employer of the bulk of the labor force, trade unions were confined to the private sector. The postwar spurt in public employment increased the importance of government as an employer, and the resulting bureaucracy and concentration of employees resulted in pressures to organize. From 1.4 million members in 1964, as public policy toward public unions was entering a new phase, public sector union membership exploded to 5.4 million in 1974, a rate of increase not witnessed since the mass unionism of the 1930s. Union membership among public employees rose as new and existent unions succeeded in organizing the expanding public sector and because 1.7 million members of employee associations were reclassified as union members in 1968. The rise of employee associations may signal another element in the classical taxonomy of union forms; to the craft and industrial modes of unionism could be added the 1970s **employee association.**

The rise of public sector unionism coincides with both a pressing "urban crisis" and a "fiscal crisis" in many metropolitan areas. The urban crisis, concerned with insufficient housing and employment as well as inadequate public services, cannot be locally attacked because of the cities' fiscal crisis, which highlights the paucity of local resources to tackle pressing local problems. The fact that public sector unionism emerged as the urban and fiscal crises received publicity leads some observers to see a cause-and-effect relationship—greedy public sector unions are indicted for contributing to the urban and fiscal crises by exercising their power for narrow parochial goals. The circumstances in which public sector unionism arose have produced some skepticism about its role in society; although most observers would guarantee public employees the right to organize and bargain with public employers, many argue that the scope of bargaining should be limited and the strike weapon banned.

As the proper role of public sector unions was debated, organizing, bargaining, and strike activity continued. While private sector bargaining was slowly being forced to accommodate the third-party interest of government, public sector bargaining was born with a government bargaining adversary. Although most public sector organizing and strike activity was (and, in some instances, remains) unlawful, public employees found that public employers were unable to resist union pressures for a variety of reasons. Unlike private employers, a public employer cannot permit public services to be discontinued indefinitely, since taxes are paid for continual provision of an (often unique) service. A public employer cannot "move" to an area with lower labor costs, since public services are locally provided. Most public services are "unique" in the sense that few inexpensive alternatives exist for such services as police and fire protection, sanitation services, or public schools. Finally, most public employers are not guaranteed permanence—periodic elections force a quick resolution of disputes and encourage public employers to make concessions whose costs are deferred until some future time.[1] The fact that elected officials must bargain with both political constituencies and public employees forces a delicate balancing act on public employers.

Although mass public sector unionism is a product of the 1960s and 1970s, public employee unions have a long history. As early as 1830, craftsmen employed by the federal government were affiliated with their private sector brethren in the mechanics', carpenters', and printers' unions. As private sector employers granted concessions, including the ten-hour workday in 1835, public employers were forced to follow suit, since they competed for the same workers.

Despite the early organization of public sector craftsmen and the founding of public employee associations in the 1880s, public employee unionism and bargaining had little impact on either public or private sector labor relations. Until 1900, government employment at federal, state, and local levels had never exceeded 1 percent of the labor force in peacetime. After an era of stability, public sector employment increased rapidly, from 3 million in 1929 (6 percent of the labor force) to 14.7 million or 16 percent of the civilian labor force in 1974. Today, most public employment is concentrated at the state and local level; in 1975, over 80 percent of all public employees were employed by state and local government (Table 8.1). Since 1960, federal employment increased 21 percent, largely because of increases in executive agency work forces, but state and local government employment nearly doubled over the same period, as the educational labor force, for example, expanded some 121 percent. Growth in government employment has been concentrated at the state and local levels, and, within the state and local sector, education has absorbed the majority of the new employees.

---

[1]Some commentators point to another difference between public and private sector labor relations—the absence of "market discipline" and profit-motivated behavior. Behavior in the private sector is usually held to be profit motivated and market constrained, that is, an employer cannot agree to *all* union demands or his product sales will decrease as consumers purchase (presumably cheaper) substitutes. In the public sector, both market discipline and the profit goal are absent. Some discipline may be imposed by taxes *if* local services are funded by local tax collections, but, more frequently, local governments derive their revenues from a variety of sources. Local public employers (often elected mayors) face both economic and political constraints. Since the public employer faces a more complex set of tradeoffs than single profit maximization, there is less certainty about public employer bargaining limits, a factor which may encourage the use of union pressures.

Table 8.1. Government Employment, 1920–1975
(thousands)

	1930	1940	1950	1960	1970	1975
Civilian labor force	49,180	55,640	62,208	69,628	82,715	91,369
Government employment	3,148	4,202	6,026	8,353	12,535	14,773
Percent	6.4	7.6	9.7	12.0	15.2	16.2
Federal employment	526	996	1,928	2,270	2,705	2,748
State and local	2,622	3,206	4,098	6,083	9,830	12,025
Education	1,173	1,327	1,680	2,816	5,109	6,228

Sources: *Employment and Earnings: Statistics for the United States, 1909–1967* (Washington, D.C.: U.S. Department of Labor, 1972). pp. 749–755, and *Employment and Earnings*, June, 1976, p. 63.

The rapid growth of employment in government made public employees ripe for unionization. Despite the late surge in public sector unionism, government employees are now more unionized than workers in the private sector. In 1955, about 1 million government employees belonged to labor organizations. Unionization proceeded slowly, reaching 1.5 million members in 1965. Between 1965 and 1975, union membership quadrupled to 6 million, claiming some 42 percent of the government work force as compared to 22 percent unionization among workers in the private sector. Government now employs about one in six workers, but within the *unionized* work force one in three workers is employed by government, reflecting the higher degree of organization in the public sector.

Reasons for the Upsurge

American distrust of despotic government traditionally limited the size and often the pay of those on the public payroll. Government service was viewed as a personal decision to exercise the people's trust, and the status and prestige of elected officials was often thought to accrue to others in government as well. In addition to job security, fringe benefits not universally granted in the private sector, and due process in grievance procedures, state and local government employees typically earned more than their private sector counterparts. In 1939, government employee earnings were 116.4 percent of average private earnings. The Civil Service Commission, established on a permanent basis in 1883, insured the privileged position of public employees by pursuing enlightened personnel policies in an era when nascent craft unions were struggling to maintain the ten-hour day.

The mass unionism of the 1930s changed the nature of private-public employment disparities, and World War II changed relative earnings positions. By 1945, employees in government were receiving wages which averaged only 88.5 percent of the all-worker average, a ratio that changed very little until the rise of public sector unionism in the mid-sixties. In the postwar era, several economic trends highlighted the advantages of unions to private sector members. With inflation, unions proved flexible in providing members with wage increases, while public employees had to await executive and legislative approval of wage increases in a time of opposition to budget deficits. Pursuit of full employment policies lessened the value of job security in the public sector, since full employment made job-search efforts relatively easy. The combination of mass unionism, inflation, and full employment eroded the privileged position once held by public employees.

In addition to the long-run equalization of conditions between public and private sector employees, several events prompted organization throughout the 1960s. Rapid increases in government employment led to bureaucracy, concentration, and impersonality in employment. While private employers were adopting new modes of personnel management, civil service procedures had made public personnel procedures relatively inflexible. Aggressive leadership, especially from the Teamsters and AFSCME, demonstrated the gains which could be secured with organization, especially when wage-price controls or guidelines were imposed and the public sector was forced into a "model" role in limiting wage increases.

Changes in public policy and public attitudes complemented the evolution of underlying trends. The idea of government as a sovereign exercising the power entrusted to it by the people retarded recognition of union rights for public employees. Under the extreme sovereign view, recognition of public employee unions would force a sharing of entrusted power with only a small segment of the populace, public employees. Rather than forming unions, the sovereignty theory held that public employees should lobby and petition for legislative changes, just as any other interest group, an idea codified in the Lloyd-LaFollette Act of 1912. The Wagner Act (NLRA) of 1935 excluded government employees from its recognition and bargaining coverage, and the Taft-Hartley Act (1947) proscribed strikes by federal employees, holding that any federal worker ". . . who strikes shall be immediately discharged from his employment." As long as the sovereignty theory of government prevailed, public employee unions could make little organizing headway.

Public Employee Organizations

At least four major types of organizations represent public employees. Two types of unions organize public employees, all-public and mixed unions. *All-public unions* draw members almost exclusively from government payrolls, at the federal, state, and/or local levels. Some of these unions, for example, the 1.1 million member American Federation of State, County, and Municipal Employees (AFSCME), are affiliated with the AFL-CIO, while others, including the National Association of Government Employees (NAGE), are independent. *Mixed unions* include both private sector and public sector employees. Most mixed unions, for example, the Service Employees International Union (SEIU), began as private sector organizations and have expanded to include, in the case of the SEIU, 30 percent public employees.

Public employees have traditionally been represented by a variety of associations. Most *public employee associations* began as lobbying organizations at the state and local levels, expanding to provide members with grievance assistance and various travel and entertainment services. Some of these state and local employee associations have merged with AFSCME (the New York Civil Service Employees Association made AFSCME the largest AFL-CIO union by joining in 1978), while others remain independent organizations.

Some groups of public employees have been members of *professional associations* long before the advent of public sector bargaining. Firefighters have been represented by an AFL-CIO union, the International Association of Fire Fighters (IAFF), for over half a century. Police officers formed nonunion associations, such as the Fraternal Order of Police (FOP), to represent their interests. Teachers have been represented by the National Education Association (NEA), nurses by the American Nursing Association, and professors by the American Association of University Professors (AAUP). As public sector bargaining spread, some of these associations began assuming union trappings, bargaining with employers and calling strikes when negotiations stalled.

No single statute governs public sector bargaining, as the NLRA and its amendments provide the framework for private sector negotiations. The result is public sector diversity. Although there are many parallels, one basic distinction is that between federal and state local bargaining. After reviewing the evolution of public sector bargaining at the federal level, we will examine the wide diversity of bargaining situations found in state and local governments.

The Federal Sector

The turning point in federal policy toward public unions came in 1962, when President Kennedy issued Executive Order 10988. To counter the fear that qualified applicants were avoiding government employment, the federal government attempted to reform federal personnel administration. Before 1962, civil service procedures regulated personnel matters and congressional actions were necessary to alter the wages and fringes of federal employees. The Kennedy order provided federal employees with the basic union rights and privileges enjoyed by private sector workers, namely, the right to organize and bargain collectively through representatives of their own choosing. Federal policy differed in two substantive areas: Management rights clauses reserved final management authority for federal employers and federal policy provided for various levels of union recognition. In addition to exclusive recognition, characteristic of the private sector, federal policy allowed organizations having at least 10 percent of the employees in a bargaining unit but failing to win a majority vote the status of "formal recognition," which confers the right of consultation in personnel matters. Employee organizations not entitled to exclusive or formal recognition were granted "informal recognition," a status which allowed only the right to have union views heard. Since virtually any employee organization could achieve some form of organization, unions of federal employees proliferated.

Between 1963 and 1967, the number of federal employees in exclusive bargaining units increased by 250 percent. Problems, not unanticipated, led to a 1967 review of federal labor policy and Executive Order 11491, issued by the Nixon administration in 1969. Bargaining rights for federal employees were reaffirmed, but the bargaining process was reorganized. An Assistant Secretary of Labor assumed responsibility for determining bargaining units, for supervising recognition procedures, and for overseeing union conduct. A Federal Labor Relations Council (FLRC) was established as an oversight agency, with final authority to determine what issues were negotiable and to hear appeals from decisions made by the Assistant Secretary of Labor. A Federal Service Impasse Panel, composed of seven nonfederal employees, was given authority to settle disputes. The scope of issues open to negotiation was broadened and criteria for bargaining unit determination were formalized, but only exclusive recognition, obtained when a union secured a majority among voting employees, remained.[2]

Union recognition and bargaining procedures among federal employees occur in a variety of contexts, from the craftsmen in the Department of Defense who follow traditional union patterns to professionals in Health, Education, and Welfare, who are concerned with agency policy as well as wages and working conditions. Although the federal government has gradually moved to permit federal employee organizations the same rights and duties as workers in the private economy, several important differences remain. The strike is prohibited and the union shop banned, often giving a union bargaining rights over far greater numbers of employees than the number of dues-paying members a union claims.[3] Federal policy has encouraged the locus of labor policy to shift from the legislative branch of government to the agency heads themselves. Although lobbying continues, decisions can now be taken at a level closer to the actual workplace.

State and Local Governments

While labor organizations were encouraged in the federal sector, state and local employee unions often faced government and popular opposition. Public employment (and taxes to finance it) has increased most rapidly in the state and local sector, with employment expansions favoring education and social ser-

---

[2]National consultation rights are permitted to labor organizations representing " . . . a substantial number of employees in the agency." The labor organization may consult with agency management on personnel matters, but the agency is only required to "carefully consider" the labor organization's view.

[3]For example, the most important federal employee union, the American Federation of Government Employees, represented some 640,000 federal workers in 1973 but claimed only 293,000 dues-paying members.

vices. Because states and even localities have different legal frameworks and attitudes toward public employee bargaining, generalization is difficult. For example, twenty states have comprehensive legal frameworks to guide public sector bargaining. Although some of these statutes are only experimental, another twenty have legislation covering particular activities (e.g., strike activity or recognition and bargaining issues), while the remaining ten states have virtually no legislation directed toward public sector unionism. Several efforts to erect a uniform national structure for public sector bargaining have been mounted, but federal regulation of state and local government labor relations appears to be an unlawful usurpation of state and local powers.[4]

Federal labor policy encouraged union activity and readily granted recognition to employee organizations. In the three state and local sectors experiencing the most union activity—education, the health care sector, and police and fire protection—strikes for recognition are frequent. As the federal government was *granting* recognition rights, teachers, nurses, and policemen were striking to obtain the same rights. Bargaining among teachers was encouraged by the successful United Federation of Teachers' (AFL-CIO) strike against New York City in 1961. Public sympathy and militancy encouraged organizational activity across the country, culminating in 312 teacher strikes between 1968 and 1970. The wave of teacher militancy encouraged efforts by health personnel, policemen and firefighters, and other local government employees to organize and press for higher wages and better working conditions.

The organizational successes of the 1960s slowed by the mid-1970s. The success of public sector unions in raising wages to 104 percent of the all-worker average increased local tax burdens, limiting public sympathy for public employees. The fiscal crises faced by some major municipalities in the mid-1970s were, in part, attributed to "excessive" past settlements with public employees. The process of recognition and bargaining at the state and local levels was streamlined and professionalized, strengthening the resolve of local administrators and legislative bodies to resist union pressures. While public sector unionism is here to stay, future organizational successes will be more difficult than those already achieved.

The State of Public Employee Unions

More than one hundred unions and associations have some government employee members, placing public employees in almost half of all labor organizations in the United States. Among federal employees, fifty-three unions

---

[4]Congressional attempts to erect a national framework for state and local bargaining procedures were declared an unconstitutional infringement of state and local powers in 1976. Some unions, including the National Education Association, favor federal standards with local participation options while others argue that federal aid should be made conditional on state and local provision of bargaining rights.

and associations are active, while state and local government workers are represented by a melange of strictly local, statewide, and national organizations. In the federal sector, hourly workers, including those of the Postal Service, are best organized. The state and local sector, by contrast, exhibits most organization among professionals in education, health, and protection in the largest cities.

In the federal sector, employees are paid on an hourly basis or are salaried. Blue-collar hourly workers in the crafts and manual occupations are most often organized by the unions representing their counterparts in the private sector. Blue-collar union membership is common; in 1970, over 80 percent of these workers were covered by negotiated agreements. Traditionally, the pay of craft and manual workers has been set at some fixed percentage (e.g., 90 percent) of the wage scale established in private sector bargaining, lower in government because of full-time work. In 1968, the Civil Service Commission established a National Wage Policy Committee, designed to ensure equal pay within an occupation across agencies and to discourage the practice of using wage comparisons when bargaining.

Employees in the Postal Service are both hourly and salaried. As the nation's largest single employer, with a 1975 labor force of nearly 700,000, or one fourth of all federal civilian employees, postal negotiations often serve as a model for other public sector unions. Despite its prohibition, the strike by 200,000 postal workers in March, 1970 prompted the Postal Reorganization Act of 1970. Article 12 of the act requires bargaining over wages and work conditions, but removed the Postal Service from Executive Order coverage and gave the NLRB jurisdiction over bargaining unit determinations and unfair labor practice charges. Although strikes and the union shop are banned, postal workers are the most organized segment of the federal labor force. The two largest unions, the American Postal Workers Union (formed by merger in 1971) and the National Association of Letter Carriers, have nearly 500,000 members but *represent* almost all the 700,000 postal employees.

Some 1.4 million federal employees are white-collar clerical, technical, or professional personnel. Wages for these employees are established by a Federal Employee Pay Council, which recommends adjustments in the eighteen-grade pay schedule. White-collar employees in government, like their private sector counterparts, are less organized than their blue-collar brethren. In 1974, the American Federation of Government Employees (AFGE) claimed over 300,000 members, nearly half of the 735,000 white-collar workers represented by unions. White-collar membership is often subdivided between professional and nonprofessional employees; in 1972, most of the organized professionals were from the Departments of Labor, Health, Education, and Welfare, the Treasury, the Army, and the Veterans Administration. Although white-collar federal employees are less organized than other federal personnel, their 50 percent organization is far greater than the 10 percent of private sector white-collar workers who are organized.

Most public employees work for state and local governments. The largest single employer is local education, employing almost one half of all state and local employees in 1974. State and local agencies are small, often employing less than fifty persons; in 1972, fewer than one in seven agencies had work forces greater than fifty. The number of different agencies to be organized (119,000 in 1972), their geographic dispersion, and the variance in legal frameworks across states and municipalities make the success of unions in the state and local area impressive. In 1972, over 20,000 written agreements were in force with 17,000 state and local agencies. Teachers (40 percent organized), policemen (56 percent), firemen (77 percent), and sanitation workers (51 percent) were best organized in 1972.

State and local government employees exhibit uneven organizational patterns. Across cities, organization is directly related to population: almost all cities of 1 million or more have municipal unions of teachers, policemen, firemen, and health care personnel. As population decreases, the degree of organization falls erratically, with teachers, policemen, and firefighters most likely to be organized in cities outside the South. To gain an appreciation for unions of state and local employees, it is useful to examine unions in education, protective services, health care, and in the remaining occupations.

Education is among the most diffused of public services in the United States. Local areas are divided into school districts, each with a (usually) elected school board. The board is responsible for setting educational policy and approving school budgets, financed by local property taxes and state and federal grants. Collective bargaining in education began with the 1961 strike by the United Federation of Teachers in New York. The success of that strike spurred teacher militancy across the country, resulting in over one third of all teachers being covered by collective bargaining agreements by 1975. The National Education Association (NEA) long dominated teacher representation, but the successes of its more militant rival, the American Federation of Teachers (AFT), prompted a changed attitude within the NEA. By 1974, the NEA, with 1.8 million members, and the AFT, with 400,000 members, had adopted such similar bargaining postures that ongoing merger talks promised a unification which would produce the nation's largest single union. Merger talks have not yet succeeded, largely because of the AFT's insistence that the new organization must retain AFL-CIO affiliation. Both unions continue organizing; the NEA in the South and West as well as in smaller cities throughout the nation and the AFT in the larger urban centers of the East and Midwest. Organization in higher education may spread even faster. Between 1968 and 1973, organization among college faculty, largely in two-year public colleges, expanded to some 80,000 members, 10 percent of all faculty. Budgetary pressures which threaten job security promise renewed organizational pressures.

Although police and fire personnel comprise only about 8 percent of all employees of state and local governments, the cost of providing police and fire protection typically exceeds one fourth of an American city's budget. Concern for public safety, the infusion of federal and state monies to combat crime, and the fraternity engendered by the unique aspects of police and fire employment have combined to make policemen and firefighters the most organized public employees in America.

Police and firemen's organizations have lobbied for better wages and working conditions since the turn of the century. The International Association of Fire Fighters (IAFF), for example, has been affiliated with the AFL-CIO since 1914. Today, it claims 150,000 members, over three fourths of all firefighters. Police unions are more fragmented; the International Conference of Police Associations (ICPA) contains local organizations representing some 200,000 policemen. The Fraternal Order of Police (FOP) is another federation of local bodies claiming 90,000 members. Other unions, including AFSCME and the Teamsters, represent some 20,000 policemen, sheriffs, and deputies.

The nation's health care system is among the most rapidly expanding sectors, employing some 2.6 million persons in 1975. Health care personnel, dominated by registered nurses (RNs), are distributed across nonprofit community hospitals (52 percent); federal, state, and local government facilities (34 percent); and proprietary (profit-making) hospitals (14 percent). Despite an early embrace of collective bargaining (1946), the American Nursing Association (ANA) has been slow to organize nurses for bargaining purposes. Even after permitting strikes in 1968 and gaining legislative approval for hospital bargaining in 1974, the ANA managed to organize only about 20 percent of all hospitals, most of them government sponsored. The ANA contains only 225,000 of the nation's 900,000 RNs, giving it fewer financial resources to wage organization and bargaining drives. Many of the concerns of nurses—the quality of patient care, the relationship between supporting personnel and doctors, and the lagging salaries of lower-level health personnel—are also of concern to other health care personnel, promising continued organizing activity.

About one half of the nation's 300,000 doctors belong to the American Medical Association (AMA). The AMA has always forced upward pressures on medical incomes by limiting the number of new doctors trained and enforcing minimum fees through county medical societies. In the mid-1970s, two events triggered bargaining and protest activity which may transform the structure of the AMA. Interns, those who have completed medical school but have not yet satisfied their working hospital residency requirements, organized and struck for higher wages and shorter hours in New York City. If interns succeed in organizing before achieving full physician status, the more militant bodies created may force the AMA to adopt new bargaining postures. Another event working to transform the AMA is the growing proportion of medical bills paid by government agencies (through Medicare and Medicaid) and insurance companies. If a national health insurance system is adopted, fees for medical services could be standardized, encouraging doctors to organize and bargain over fee schedules.

Issues in Public Sector Bargaining

The explosion in public sector unionism in the 1960s left federal, state, and local governments ill prepared to face the array of labor issues which arose. The federal government, which encouraged organization and (limited) negotiations, was best prepared, but state and local governments were neither prepared nor capable of confronting the myriad labor issues which arose. These issues fall in three broad classes: (1) organizing rights and procedures (e.g., should public employees be governed by separate labor relations statutes?); (2) bargaining process issues, including bargaining unit determination, the scope of bargaining, and the role of supervisory personnel in public sector unions; and (3) impasse procedures (i.e., the right of public employees to strike). The way these issues are resolved promises to shape the ultimate character of public sector labor relations.

One of the most intractable public sector issues must be confronted at the outset—just who does the union bargain with? In the private sector, the employer is readily identifiable, but the merging of the executive and legislative branches in many local governments makes it unclear whether the mayor or the city council is ultimately responsible for acting as the employer. In theory, the employer is the government branch or agency which has decision-making authority, but this authority is often diffused (e.g., in the federal government, agency heads make personnel decisions in accord with civil service procedures, but Congress reserves the right to increase wages and fringe benefits). The resulting fragmentation in public sector employer responsibility permits (and often forces) public sector unions to bargain for change with one negotiator and lobby for change with another body.

The determination of management responsibility is complicated by the absence of comprehensive public sector labor relations laws in many states. States with such laws often help to define the bargaining relationship by delineating lines of employer authority. But the array of public services provided raises issues about the generality of any public sector statute—is a separate public sector statute necessary, and, if it is, should the state enact separate statutes for each type of public service, such as one law for police and fire protection, one for education, and another for health services? States have adopted different views on this issue. Some states have only one comprehensive statute, some have separate statutes, and others have no public sector labor statutes. Some states have created separate administrative agencies (e.g., Public Employee Relations Boards) to oversee public sector bargaining, while others rely on one administrative agency to govern labor relations in both the private and public sectors. Diversity among (and within) states arises from differences of opinion about the organizational and bargaining rights of public employees as well as distinctive approaches to providing those rights.

After public employees are granted organizing and bargaining rights, pragmatic issues remain. In the private sector, bargaining units (each of which has a labor contract) are formed on the basis of "communities of interest." If the work force is relatively specialized, with defined skills or distinctive work patterns, the result is normally a variety of smaller bargaining units. But if the "community of interest" is construed to dominate any local departmental interests, bargaining units can be quite large, including, for instance, an entire auto plant.

Public sector unit determination generally turns on this issue of large versus small. Most current public sector bargaining units are very small (typically ten to forty employees), since few public sector agencies are large. Small units are usually thought to provide more room for individual self-determination, but they also result in fragmentation, increasing the costs of bargaining. Larger units, while permitting the public employer to centralize bargaining, are often thought to limit the degree to which individuals feel that self-government accompanies organization, since bargaining is conducted between two centralized (and often distant) groups. Despite the ambiguity in determining an optimal unit size, there has been a marked tendency toward larger bargaining units in the public sector.[5]

Closely related to bargaining unit determination is the problem of supervisory personnel in public sector unions. In the private sector, the NLRA states that "any individual having authority . . . to hire, transfer, suspend, lay off, recall, promote, discharge, assign, reward or discipline other employees" is defined as a supervisor and excluded from union membership. In the public sector, the term "supervisor" is used more loosely, and public sector supervisors may have very little discretionary authority over employees. Three resolutions to the supervisor issue can be observed. In some areas, supervisors and their employees are in the same bargaining unit (e.g., education and firefighting). In other areas, supervisors are organized, but in separate bargaining units and sometimes in different unions from their employees. Finally, in some areas, supervisors do not care to or are prohibited from organization. The role of the supervisor is especially contentious because the supervisor is often responsible for implementing the contract and acting as the management representative in grievance procedures, prompting fears of divided loyalties when the supervisor and his subordinates are in the same union.

After bargaining units are determined and bargaining representatives are selected, another issue looms—just what can the union negotiate? Can teachers bargain over class size and textbooks in addition to wages and hours? Can social workers bargain over the number of clients each serves or the level of client benefits? Determining the proper scope of public sector bargaining is difficult because public sector employees often demand a voice in setting departmental or agency policies and programs. Teachers, for example, may want to bargain over those factors which contribute to a "quality education," even though the school board argues that educational policy is *its* responsibility. Determining the *scope* of public sector bargaining is of concern to both unions (and public employees), public employers, and the taxpaying and service-consuming public.

In the private sector, the law divides bargaining subjects into mandatory, permissible (or voluntary), and prohibited classes. Failure to bargain over mandatory bargaining subjects (or pressure to bargain over proscribed clauses) can

---

[5]See, for example, Ralph Jones, *Public Sector Labor Relations* (Washington, D.C.: Contract Research Corporation, 1976), pp. 21–53.

lead to unfair labor practice charges. The intermediate, permissible class of bargaining subjects is most vulnerable to change; in general, the number of permissible subjects over which private sector parties bargain is contingent on relative bargaining power (although a union cannot strike to force concessions on permissible bargaining subjects).

In the public sector, one widely held view argues that the scope of bargaining must be constrained, since bargaining between public employers and unions eliminates any citizen input into such questions as classroom sizes or welfare caseloads. To prevent public policies from being unduly impacted by collective bargaining, many states have attempted to restrict the subjects open to public sector bargaining, to limit bargaining duties on some topics to "meet and confer" rather than "collectively negotiate." Although the real impact of such restrictions is in doubt (some unions may simply lobby or publicize their demands on restricted bargaining issues), there is considerable sentiment for restricting the scope of public sector bargaining because of an overriding *public* interest, an interest which may be neglected or shunted aside in union-employer negotiations.

Why is there so much interest in "assisting" the public employer? The answer revolves around the burning issue in public sector bargaining, the role of the strike and public employer vulnerability to strike pressures. In the private sector, bargaining power was defined as the ability to inflict costs *or* to "take" the costs the bargaining adversary could impose, but these were largely *economic* costs, that is, lost wages and foregone profits. In the public sector, goods are not produced for profit, and, although striking public sector employees are sacrificing wages, it is the public, a "third-party neutral," which bears the inconvenience of foregoing services for which *it* pays.[6] The twin issues of public inconvenience and public employees striking to (unlawfully) appropriate power delegated to elected officials account for the pre-1969 ban on public sector strikes in all states.

Despite the strike ban, public employee strikes occurred, as teachers, policemen, and firefighters were able to secure gains and freedom from retribution for striking. But the disruptions caused by public sector strikes prompted widespread interest in strike alternatives, especially for workers providing "essential" public services. If all public services are grouped by their "essential nature," this approach would substitute binding arbitration for strikes in "critical services" such as police and fire protection; permit strikes (subject to injunction) in "essential services," including hospitals, schools, and sanitation; and give other public employees the same right to strike as that enjoyed by private sector workers. Other strike alternatives include **mediation** and **fact finding,** or compulsory interest arbitration, through which disputed issues in contract negotiations can be appealed to an outside neutral.

---

[6]Strikes in the private sector, especially in such areas as transportation or communication industries, can also impose (inconvenience) costs on the public, but the public does not pay for such services as airline flights not taken.

As public policy attempts to define public employee rights and find strike substitutes, public sector strikes continue apace. In 1974, over 161,000 public employees were involved in 384 public sector strikes, largely (91 percent of all strikes and 85 percent of all striking workers) in local governments. Illegal strikes, especially by those charged with upholding the law (e.g., policemen and sheriffs), as well as the ability of a city to "take" a strike and survive, have produced a *de facto* right to strike by default. Although union leaders can (and are) still jailed for not enjoining their members to return to work, most charges of unlawful activity are quickly dropped at the conclusion of any strike activity.

American governments at federal, state, and local levels are searching for policies which respect both individual rights and the public interest. In other nations, governments have had more experience with public sector unionism, since European nations usually have a larger proportion of the labor force in public employment and because public employment is often viewed much like private employment. Although distinctive legal traditions, differing political systems, and varying ideological factors have made each nation's labor policies toward public employees unique, several patterns can be discerned. In most European nations (and in the United States), public sector employees are better organized than those in the private sector.[7] In England, for example, 75 percent of all public employees are organized, compared to a meager 30 percent organization rate in the private sector. In Germany, the public organization rate of 75 percent overshadows the 25 percent private organization rate, as does France's 46 percent organization in the public sector. Although public employment is more significant in Europe, the locus of employment is still in the private sector, placing most union members in the private sectors despite a higher degree of public sector organization.

Attitudes toward public employee bargaining and strike activity vary widely. Government sometimes acts as a "model employer," as in Britain at the turn of the century, and public employees enjoy bargaining rights similar to those accorded private sector workers. In Germany, the special status of civil servants and the highly centralized bargaining procedure limit the number of bargaining subjects, leading to local unrest and the first nationwide strike of public employees in 1974. Sweden permits its public employees to strike, but the Swedish policy of attempting to narrow wage differentials between low- and high-wage workers has exacerbated tensions between better-paid public sector workers and private sector workers. In contrast to European acceptance of public employee unions, Japan has proscribed public employee strikes and sought to avoid dealings with existing public employee unions. The result has

---

[7]The most comprehensive source of information on public sector unionism in other nations is a series of country monographs edited by R. A. Smith and C. M. Rehmus of the University of Michigan (Institute of Labor and Industrial Relations, 1971 and 1972). A convenient summary of the series is J. Goldberg, "Public Employee Labor Relations in Other Democracies—A Review Essay," *Monthly Labor Review,* October, 1972, pp. 37–43.

been a mixture of labor peace and unrest, as some public employees accepted traditional paternalism in government while others, including the teachers' union, have sought to achieve gains through both bargaining and political activity.

What is the long-term significance of public sector unionism? Will public sector unionism inject a political element into American labor relations? Answers are not yet available, but the growing importance of (especially state and local) government employment promises to keep public employee unionism near the center of dynamic union activity for at least another decade. As bureaucracy and impersonality produce a desire for public sector unionization, the need to balance tax revenues and government expenditures in a time of demands for expanded public services will make unions appear as attractive advocates for public employees.

Summary

Public employee unionism is the most dynamic sector of union activity. Largely a product of the 1960s and 1970s, public sector unions and employee associations now represent a majority of the nation's 15 million public employees. Organizing successes in the public sector resulted from the encouragement given organization in the federal government, growing numbers and increased bureaucracy in public employment, and evidence that public sector unions were able to provide their members real wage and employment benefits.

Most public sector unions and most unionized public employees work for state and local governments, since such governments employ 80 percent of all public employees. Organization and bargaining efforts vary across states and cities, but three public services—education, police and fire protection, and health services—have experienced considerable organization, especially in the larger cities. Education, which accounts for over half of all state and local work forces, contains the largest number of unionized public employees.

Public employee bargaining is more complex than private sector negotiation because of the unique issues which arise. After bargaining units are determined and the role of supervisory personnel in public employee unions is settled, the union must still ascertain: (1) who its bargaining adversary is, and (2) what subjects are open to negotiation. States and cities vary in their definitions of public employer and in the range of bargaining topics open to discussion, but unions have been able to obtain agreements which deal with both wages and broadly defined employment conditions, including such issues as limitations on class size in schools and the proper number of clients in social services.

Public sector bargaining began (especially at state and local levels) before any legal regulative framework had been established. In many states organization was illegal, and all states proscribed strikes until 1969. Although public employee strikes are still banned in most states and cities, strikes occur, disrupting local public services. The inconvenience engendered by these strikes as well as their dubious lawfulness has prompted a search for strike alternatives, including binding arbitration, mediation, or simple permission to strike, depending on the "essential nature" of the service provided. As government employment continues to increase, public sector unionism promises to be a prime area of union strength.

Bibliography

Smith, R., et al. *Labor Relations Law in the Public Sector*. New York: Bobbs-Merrill Company, 1974.

The best guide to the legal aspects of public sector unionism.

Stieber, J. *Public Employee Unionism: Structure, Growth, and Policy*. Washington, D.C.: The Brookings Institution, 1973.

A detailed study of the government and bargaining strategies of public sector unions.

Wellington, H., and R. Winter. *The Unions and the Cities*. Washington, D.C.: The Brookings Institution, 1971.

An assessment of the applicability of private sector bargaining rights in the public sector which argues that the extension of the right to strike provides public unions with "excessive" bargaining power.

Contemporary Labor Issues

9

Unions emerged as protective institutions, designed to insulate members from the disruptions which accompany change in a market economy. Initially rejected and stifled, unions were forced to struggle for acceptance. A generation ago, public policy embraced unions and collective bargaining as the "best" way to resolve labor conflict and promote labor peace, marking a new turn in American labor relations. Unions flourished and matured, collective bargaining increased in scope and complexity, the economic growth continued on its uneven but upward path.

Today new pressures confront labor relations. Union membership has not kept pace with the growth of the labor force, and collective bargaining is increasingly constrained by intervention in both its processes and outcomes. The economic impact of unions is sometimes viewed as detrimental to economic policies, prompting a defensive union reaction. As the labor force grows in size and sophistication, new demands for participation emerge, demands which unions are ill-suited to meet. The net result of these new pressures may be the evolution of unions with broader socioeconomic goals. The labor union of the future may turn to the political process to achieve these broader goals and confine collective bargaining to the promotion of its narrow economic interests.

The Labor Relations Agenda

The American labor movement faces continuing challenges on several fronts. Between 1974 and 1976, the number of union members declined by nearly 1 million. The primary purpose of American unions, collective bargaining, is subject to ever more constraints, as previously excluded parties impose their influence on both the processes and outcomes of collective bargaining. The final issue is more speculative. In a modern industrial welfare state, what is the "proper" role of labor unions—should they be expected to represent the broad interests of the "working class" or do they evolve into narrow interest groups? In this section, we examine the potential size and instruments used by American labor unions.

American labor unions grew from 16 million members in the early 1960s to a high-water mark of 20 million in 1974 (U.S. members). Over the same period, the labor force increased much faster, from 72 million to 93 million, causing the union share of the total labor force to fall from 24 to 20 percent. The labor force promises to continue growing at a rapid rate, forcing the union share of the labor force to fall further. What does the decrease in union membership portend? Despite recent stagnation and decline, the longer-term prospects for union growth appear promising, as members are added in several areas.

Most of the decrease in union membership between 1974 and 1976 was a direct result of the economic recession, illustrating union dependence on the economy. Most of the union membership loss occurred in manufacturing, where employment dropped by 2 million and union membership decreased by 700,000. This recession-induced membership loss is probably temporary, since union membership will increase when currently unemployed workers return to their old jobs.

Another immediate source of new union members are the 3 million state and local public employees in associations, as, for example, the 1.8 million teachers in the National Education Association. As more of these associations assume union trappings, engaging in collective bargaining and striking and picketing to encourage acceptance of their demands, their "nonunion" status will become even more artificial. Since these employee associations have grown at a rate of more than 8 percent annually between 1968 and 1976, and because 5 million state and local government employees are not yet represented by any union or association, association growth and transformation[1] promise to provide the labor movement with a significant share of its new members in the coming decade.

A third union frontier is among "low-wage" workers in both the private and public sectors, primarily in the South and in rural areas. In many urban areas, organizing drives among relatively low-paid health care personnel, sanitation workers, and social service workers during the 1960s and 1970s were remarkably successful. But remaining concentrations of unorganized workers are in the traditionally nonunion South and in rural America. It is in these areas that manufacturing employment, a traditional source of union members, is

---

[1]Existing associations are largely comprised of state and local government employees. Other possible sources of "union" members are the professional associations of doctors (especially interns), and university professors. New York City interns succeeded in obtaining revised work schedules after organization and strike activity in 1975, and promise continued organized pressures in the future. Although the self-employed doctors of the American Medical Association (AMA) will probably be "excluded" from bargaining unless national health insurance makes them government employees, doctors already act to effectively fix minimum fee schedules.

University professors have traditionally resisted activites which smack of bargaining. In recent years, however, the American Association of University Professors (AAUP) has instituted a lobbying program at several state legislatures, and more militant state and junior colleges have been organized by groups as diverse as AFSCME and the Teamsters. To date, only a small fraction of the 650,000 faculty in institutions of higher learning have been organized.

growing fastest, but unions have not been successful in organizing these workers. Some manufacturers, especially in the textile industry, have preferred to
resist unions, even if the resistance is unlawful and results in fines rather than
recognize and bargain with unions.

Unions argue that NLRB delays and unlawful employer actions are responsible for frustration in these organizing drives. In 1977, a labor law reform to
expedite NLRB procedures and to impose new penalties on unlawful employer actions was proposed. The legislation, aimed (in part) at the antiunion
tactics of some southern textile companies, would require the NLRB to hold an
election within seventy-five days of the date that the union submits the required
number of signed authorization cards (30 percent of all employees). Under the
proposed law, the NLRB would be expanded to expedite hearings on unfair
labor practice charges since, in most instances, it is the *employer* who benefits
from delays.[2] Finally, the proposed legislation would permit quicker court enforcement of NLRB decisions and permit new penalties against employers, including retroactive pay for *all* workers if the employer unlawfully delays a
contract agreement and a suspension of federal contracts for employers who
willfully violate labor laws. The exact form of the final reform measure remains
uncertain, but some labor law reform appears inevitable.[3]

Economic recovery, the growth and transformation of associations, and
labor law reforms all promise to augment labor union membership. But the
fastest-growing class of workers, white-collar employees outside government,
remain largely unorganized. Despite a concentration of numbers, bureaucracy,
and organizing drives, white-collar worker organization is largely confined to
those in clerical jobs. Two of the largest white-collar occupations, teachers and
engineers, each with about 1.2 million members, illustrate the difference between public and private sector white-collar organization. While public sector
teachers were being organized, engineers, after a brief flurry of organizing activity in the early 1960s, have remained largely unorganized despite growing
competition, the lesser status accorded engineers as the Sputnik challenge
fades, and the boom or bust nature of engineering employment. Experience in

---

[2]Some observers see evidence of renewed employer opposition to unions in the new labor-
management consulting firms. These firms are sometimes hired to keep a firm nonunion by oppos-
ing the union at the outset of organizing activity. The result has been a rash of unfair labor practice
charges, 15,000 charging that discriminatory employer actions unlawfully ''chilled'' union activity
[Section 8(a)3] in fiscal 1976. If the union does win the election (unions have won 53 percent of the
97,680 NLRB-conducted elections between 1956 and 1974), these consultants sometimes counsel
delay in signing the initial contract or encourage decertification elections.

[3]In addition to labor law reform, a series of corporate law revisions have been proposed. The
federal government possesses the legal power to enforce minimum standards of corporate conduct
in employment practices (through, for example, affirmative action and safety laws), in marketing
and sales strategies (antitrust laws), and in dealings with shareholders and political figures (largely
through Securities and Exchange Commission regulations). Revised and expanded employee rights
could result from the extension of minimum standards legislation or by the replacement of diverse
state corporate charters with a comprehensive federal charter. For an assessment of the feasibility
and impacts of corporate law reform see J. Liberman, ''New Fire in the Drive to Reform Corporation Law,'' *Business Week*, November 21, 1977, pp. 98–100.

both America and Europe demonstrates the organizability of white-collar workers, but this same experience shows that unionism is most closely associated with white-collar *public* employees. (In Europe, a much larger proportion of the white-collar work force is employed by government.)

The forces common to organization in all the recent areas of union growth have been impersonality and scarcity. Increasing the number of employees increases the distance between supervisor and workers, just as a renewed "scarcity consciousness," resulting from the influx of young adults into the labor force at a time when pundits proclaim a new era of scarcity, generates a new respect for some traditional union institutions. When (good) jobs are scarce, they must be rationed, and the union rule of seniority often seems preferable to unilateral employer assessments of ability. Similarly, the remoteness of superiors can make a uniform, negotiated wage superior to individual "merit" determinations for many employees. If scarcity consciousness takes hold in America, we may witness a revival of both unions and union institutions.

Prospects for union growth appear favorable, but the future of the traditional union instrument and purpose, collective bargaining, is more clouded. Collective bargaining is a rare institution. Developed by workers and employers to accommodate felt needs (and not part of any of the various utopian societies which have been proposed), it has proved a resilient and flexible means to accommodate labor conflict and promote labor cooperation. But collective bargaining is being expanded to include more topics and to permit "outside" parties to intervene. The expansion of bargaining topics is largely union inspired, as the union seeks to bargain over job rights and new benefits, such as dental and legal insurance, day-care facilities, and extended educational leaves. The voices and influences of third parties, on the other hand, are heard and felt because of government intervention in the bargaining process and in bargaining outcomes.

Government intervention in bargaining outcomes usually occurs in times of macroeconomic stress, most frequently when public policy is attempting to limit wage and price increases. Intervention can assume two forms—wage and price "freezes," during which the union bargaining role is superfluous, and wage-price guidelines, under which wages and prices are permitted to rise within defined bounds. Unions (and many employers) usually resist this intervention because it denies them the bargaining and pricing freedom they feel they require. Unions have a more parochial concern; if public policy is going to determine "permissible" wage increases, what role is left for the union? Although the union can still serve as workplace advocate in grievance procedures, its usefulness is eroded without an effective bargaining function.

Intervention in bargaining outcomes is usually confined to temporary periods of economic crisis. Intervention in the bargaining process, however, is more permanent. The collective bargaining interaction is a relationship between the employer and the union, permitting the parties to exclude other interests. But what if the union and the employer agree, for example, to exclude Blacks or women? If bargaining outcomes are not subject to review, then Blacks and women may be denied employment or promotion opportunities in certain industries because of the (government-encouraged) process of collective bargaining.

To remedy the biases and exclusions which may result from collective bargaining, government has begun intervening in the bargaining process. As the parties bargain, they are constrained by a variety of laws governing equal pay (Equal Pay Act), nondiscrimination by race, sex, age, or religion (Civil Rights Act and Age Discrimination in Employment Act), health and safety standards (Occupational Safety and Health Act—OSHA), and pension and retirement plan standards (Employee Retirement Income Security Act—ERISA). These constraints serve to protect minority and future interests, but they also place new strains on the bargaining process. A society devoted to largely "free" collective bargaining may be forced to protect some rights through social welfare legislation rather than through collective bargaining.

The impact of the changed environment for union growth and collective bargaining is mixed. Unions will not disappear; indeed, they appear more likely to grow in numbers rather than decline. But the instruments used by unions will be subject to increasing constraint, largely because the parties will be forced to accommodate previously neglected views. The net result may be a flourishing institution which asserts itself as much in the political as in the economic arena, a subject to which we will return.

The Economic Impact of Unions

Labor unions exist, in large part, to secure economic gains for their members. But the success of unions in securing economic gains has ramifications which go beyond the union members and the employer involved. If the United Steelworkers of America and the steel industry agree to "excessive" wage increases, the result may be steel price increases which, in turn, translate into price increases for a variety of items fabricated from steel. As the price increases spread throughout the economy, the nation is faced with the familiar policy dilemma of how to slow rising prices without increasing unemployment.

The economic impact of unions occurs at two distinct levels. At the level of the individual company or industry, the union secures wage increases which can affect production costs and hence prices and sales. But union power at the company or industry level is constrained by market forces. If the union succeeds in driving production costs too high, sales will fall and, ultimately, employment and union membership will decrease. Although some unions are willing to accept less employment in exchange for high wages (e.g., in longshoring and mining), most unions attempt to balance wage demands against any adverse employment (and hence union membership) effects. Thus, in the private economy, the market serves to discipline the economic power of unions.

Even if the market serves to discipline union-management interaction, labor agreements can have broader economic impacts. Unions represent only a minority of the labor force, but decisions made in the union sector can be transmitted to the nonunionized sector if union and nonunion firms compete for the same workers. In addition to direct wage impacts, unions can erect barriers to entry, keeping potential workers from jobs in some industries and maintaining higher wages.

The economic impact of unions is a subject of intense debate. Since World War II, almost all industrial nations have been faced with the seemingly incompatible goals of simultaneously achieving full employment and maintaining stable prices without massive government intervention in the economy. Policy making is difficult because no single theory is available to explain the causes of unemployment and inflation. The economic impact of unions revolves around the extent to which unions are responsible for inflation, since inflation is what gives rise to the restrictive governmental policies which perpetrate unemployment.

The union impact on wage levels in particular industries is usually examined by comparing the wages of union and nonunion workers in a comparable industry or by examining wage increases before and after union organization. Wages increase both with and without unions. What these studies seek to examine is the extent to which unions increase wages more than simple market forces would, that is, the extent to which unions increase the *relative* wages of union members. The problem with empirical studies is that it is very difficult to find workers who are otherwise identical except for union membership. The comparison of wage increases before and after unionization is often clouded because of other economic factors which operate to alter wage levels (e.g., wages will rise in inflationary times with or without union representation).

In the most comprehensive study of the union impact on relative wages, it was found that unions have an average wage effect of 0 to 25 percent; that is, union wages were 100 to 125 percent of those received by nonunion workers. Surprisingly, the greatest union impact on relative wages was found during the depression years, when unions were found to have increased member wages about 25 percent. In the inflationary period after World War II, the union impact was minimal, between 0 and 5 percent. The explanation for this apparent paradox, which finds unions strongest when prices are falling and weakest when prices are rising, is the wage rigidity which often characterizes payment practices. In unionized sectors, the labor agreement fixes wages for a period of time, usually two or three years. In nonunion sectors, by contrast, wages are free to respond to changes in the labor market. Thus, in a period of recession or depression, the excess supply of labor can force real wages downward in the nonunionized sector (i.e., when wages rise less than prices). In inflationary times, the reverse occurs as nonunion employers discover they must bid up wages to attract workers while union members are "locked in" to employment at a previously agreed upon wage.

The union impact on wages is not confined to wage levels alone. Unions also act to change wage differentials between industries and between jobs. In some industries, such as mining, construction, longshoring, and trucking, unions have significantly raised wages over what they would have been in the absence of unions by restricting the supply of labor. In other industries, including apparel and textiles, the union impact has been far less substantial. In almost all industries, the unions have attempted to overcome the handicap imposed by rising prices by negotiating cost-of-living clauses in recent contracts. These clauses protect union members by insuring that wages keep pace with the cost of living.

If the union impact on relative wages is small and variable across industries, how can unions be identified as a major culprit in recent inflation? Union culpability for inflation arises from a particular view about how inflationary pressures are generated. If the economy is composed of different sectors, and union strength is confined to only several sectors, then the impact of unions depends on (1) the union impact within unionized sectors, and (2) the way in which price increases are transmitted between sectors. If, for example, unions in the steel industry succeed in increasing wages, thus forcing steel price increases, and if the steel industry itself has enough monopoly power to pass on the price increases to its customers, then we could say that the steelworkers' union has contributed, in part, to rising prices in nonorganized industries. But the critical element in this theory is the transmission mechanism, that is, the steel industry itself must have monopoly power to free itself from market discipline and pass the wage-induced price increases on to *its* customers. Thus, it would appear that union inflationary pressures are possible only if unionized employers also have some monopoly power.

Even the limited economic power of unions may be sufficient to induce government intervention into the wage and price setting mechanism. In the 1960s, government intervened in the results of collective bargaining by "jawboning," or pressuring unions and management to hold wage and price increases within productivity-determined bounds. In 1971, the seemingly intractable conundrum of inflation and unemployment prompted a wage-price freeze. Both guideposts and freezes are, naturally, opposed by unions and management, since they substitute public decisions for private decisions.

As long as the unemployment-inflation dilemma confronts the nation, the culpability of unions for the economic dilemma will be debated. Most economists would agree that some unions in particular industries and situations are able to exert significant influences on member wages, obtaining wage increases which can then be passed through to the customers of that industry. But the impact of such union power on the broader economy is unclear. Even if we could show that this union impact was significant in particular situations, it must be recognized that the problem has a dual nature. It is not simply union power to raise wages but also the power of businesses to pass on price increases which ultimately results in inflation.

Workers' Participation and the Quality of Work

The introduction of collective bargaining assured workers a voice in determining their own wages and working conditions. But workers are concerned with more than just wages and working conditions; they are also interested in the structure of work, management plans, and, especially in the public sector, the purposes and goals of the agency (or company) in which they work. Workers' participation plans are devices through which worker representatives are provided management positions, giving them continuing access to and influence over company policy. Quality of work or humanization plans, which seek to make work a "good" itself rather than merely a means to earn the income necessary to enjoy "goods," may be associated with a workers' participation plan or be completely independent of worker participation.

The most widely discussed workers' participation plan is the codetermination *(Mitbestimmung)* introduced in the West German coal and steel industry in 1951. The codetermination plan was a response to worker demands for a voice in management as well as a response to pressures for intervention in companies which had assisted Hitler's war efforts. Under the law, all coal and steel companies with 1,000 or more employees must reserve one half of their board of supervisors positions (equivalent to an American board of directors) for worker representatives. The worker and management representatives jointly select a neutral chairman, who casts the deciding vote in the event of a deadlock. In other German companies with more than 2,000 employees, elected worker representatives comprise one-third of the board of supervisors.

How much real "participation" does the German scheme provide? German unions generally praise their system, pointing to specific decisions which the worker representatives were able to influence or reverse. Foreign observers are far less enthusiastic, often viewing participation as more apparent than real. Some note that the board of supervisors meets only four or five times annually, that worker representatives are often incapable of understanding the complexities of management problems, or that management can sometimes manipulate the worker representatives by controlling the flow of information to them.

Despite some academic skepticism, the drive for workers' participation continues unabated. In 1976, the German government extended "parity participation" (half workers and half management) to large companies outside steel and coal but reserved one worker seat for a senior management official, assuring a management victory in the event of a deadlock. Sweden adopted a form of workers' participation in 1976, and some developing countries (Iran, for example) are attempting to mitigate the pains of industrialization with a workers' participation scheme.

European experiments with direct worker participation in management have not been embraced by the American labor movement. American unions, accustomed to bargaining with management, fear that worker representatives would have "split loyalties," seeking to accommodate both worker and management needs. Rather than seeking seats on boards of directors, American unions are more prone to push for an expansion in the scope of collective bargaining, seeking to force employer bargaining over any major decisions which would affect the existence or structure of jobs.[4] Although the push for participation is

---

[4]Expanding the scope of bargaining reserves, of course, a much larger role for the union in "participation." Worker representatives are usually elected from among *all* workers, union and

likely to continue, it is unclear whether such participation will utilize the existing collective bargaining institution or adopt a direct worker representation role.

The drive for increased participation in decisions affecting work is closely intertwined with a concern for the quality of work itself. Since the advent of factory production, work has been viewed as "bad," something which was done only for the (monetary) rewards it provided. This view of work and individual psychology resulted in management carrot-and-stick approaches to worker motivation—that is, ensure worker efforts by providing the means to enjoy nonwork time and threaten discipline and discharge for insufficient effort.

The rise of unionism and protective labor laws has given workers certain employment rights, rights which increased the costs of hiring and firing workers. As production processes became more complex, employers began to realize that discharge was an expensive disciplinary device, since each new worker had to undergo costly training. This combination of changed employment practices and increasingly costly labor turnover led to an *employer* interest in alternative forms of worker motivation.

As in many other labor areas, Sweden was among the pioneers in work "humanization." While supervisory personnel and most white-collar workers had long been thought to derive some satisfaction from their work, the routine of the assembly line worker epitomized the monotonous work where worker dissatisfaction was thought to be pandemic. According to the "scientific management" precepts of Frederick Taylor at the turn of the century, efficiency in production and worker satisfaction are simultaneously achieved if each worker performs several (simple) tasks over and over again, as on an automobile assembly line. The Swedes were among the first to attempt automobile production with modified assembly line procedures, in which teams of workers assemble a complete automobile (or at least a substantial part of the whole product), with teams of workers collectively determining job assignments. As with all such experiments, two questions are vital: (1) do the changed production procedures result in better worker morale, and (2) are the alternative production arrangements economically feasible; that is, are the alternative production methods profitable enough to induce employers voluntarily to redesign the work process?

The rationale behind work humanization is based on the psychological premise that workers *want* their work to be interesting, to be creative rather than routine, to be "meaningful."[5] It is assumed that workers are willing to make some tradeoffs between wages and work quality, with affluence and rising levels of education causing the quality of work to loom larger in employ-

---

nonunion, allowing worker participation to be independent of the union. If all demands are funneled through the union, the union retains its primary representation role.

[5]The most comprehensive advocacy of work redesign is found in *Work in America: Report of a Special Task Force to the Secretary of HEW* (Cambridge, Mass.: M.I.T. Press, 1972). For a skeptical review, see H. Wool, "What's Wrong with Work in America?" *Monthly Labor Review*, March, 1973, pp. 38–44. Another skeptical view, which characterizes quality of work notions as "the foreman in the pink jumpsuit," is found in A. Weber, "The Changing Environment in Industrial Relations," 20th Anniversary Symposium, Michigan State University, November 4–5, 1976.

ment choices. But the evidence of worker discontent from "job satisfaction" surveys is ambiguous at best; those very dissatisfied with work are often offset by those who proclaim satisfaction with current work arrangements. The real test, often overlooked, is, for example, worker preferences for additional wages versus job redesign—would most workers be willing to surrender part of a wage increment in exchange for redesigned jobs? Because the exact degree of worker dissatisfaction *before* work rearrangement is unclear, the impact of humanizing work on morale is difficult to gauge.[6] Until workers adjust to the redesigned jobs, they may find conventional production methods, such as the auto assembly line, preferable to the "work team" alternatives.[7]

If the impacts of changed work environments on worker morale are difficult to assess, their economic feasibility is easier to examine. European experiments with altered assembly line procedures were frequently induced by government subsidies with little observed impact; the newer plants do not seem to be more or less profitable.[8] The fact that new production arrangements are cheapest to incorporate when plants are constructed suggests that work environments will change as plant construction occurs, an evolutionary process.

The long-term importance of work humanization efforts is hard to assess because we have such an incomplete understanding of the psychology of individual well-being. The need for work satisfaction is assumed to derive from a hierarchical ordering of human needs. These needs, according to psychologist Abraham Maslow, begin with basic material requisites such as food and shelter, ascend to higher levels, such as self-esteem, and, eventually demand "self-actualization" in work. One difficulty with this method of viewing worker well-being is that it ignores interdependencies; even if basic wants are satisfied, will the drive for material possessions (and the wages necessary to obtain them) cease if others ("the Joneses") continue purchasing material things? If the theory requires that individuals must first fulfill more basic wants than others in their comparison group, then no relatively egalitarian society will ever produce a working class which aspires to self-actualization.

Perhaps the most important determinant of the degree to which work changes are wrought will be the availability of workers. If workers evince dissatisfaction with auto assembly work by "voting with their feet" and seeking other employment, auto manufacturers will be forced to redesign work to at-

---

[6]Even if absenteeism and turnover decline in "humanized" work environments, it is hard to find statistical proof which makes the changed work environment responsible. If the desire for good jobs varies across workers, then lower observed attributes of work dissatisfaction in humanized environments may simply reflect self-selectivity; that is, workers to whom job quality is important will seek out and take such jobs. If the work environment is changed for *all* workers, aggregate absenteeism and turnover may decline only marginally or not at all.

[7]American workers who were temporarily employed at a Swedish auto plant which had substituted team production of whole autos for the repetitive tasks required on a conventional auto assembly line expressed a preference for the conventional system because it demanded less concentration while working. See *New York Times,* January 5, 1975, Part IV, p. 11.

[8]See "Another Way of Making Cars," *The Economist,* December 26, 1976, pp. 68–69.

tract workers, provided wage increases are insufficient to attract enough employees. Some industries may be able to maintain unpleasant jobs in otherwise defunct industries by relying on foreign workers; indeed, many of the work humanization programs in Europe were prompted by the reluctance of natives to accept auto assembly and other menial jobs. Rather than the psychological drives of individuals, the *quantity* of labor may prove to be of greatest import in determining the extent of future work humanization efforts.

The Future of Unionism

Unions emerged as controversial institutions and remain controversial today. Controversy about unions is found in society at large, which asks whether unions are "good" or "bad," and within the labor movement itself, where the debate is between advocates of a broader-based labor movement and more pragmatic-minded "business unionists." The social utility of unionism is a matter of individual decision, but the proper goals and purposes of unions are subject to study. While we cannot answer the debate here, the outlines of the extreme positions can be delineated.

Unions emerged as protective devices to counter the disruptions which are omnipresent in any dynamic society. Initially, unions sought to protect both members and the broader "working class" from the dislocations imposed by industrialization. As unionism spread, workers were guaranteed rights in employment as well as representation in bargaining over wages with an employer. Nonunion employers often accepted union-won wages and employment rights, and public policy incorporated a number of union-advocated employment and income rights in the development of the modern welfare state. As the state assumes more responsibility for both the poor and the working class, what role remains for socially conscious labor unions?

Some critics argue that unions become redundant in a modern welfare state, that society can ensure employee rights with protective labor laws and guarantee (minimal) economic and social benefits through economic and social policies. While acknowledging the usefulness of unions during industrialization, when unions protected worker rights, these critics see unions acting as narrow interest groups in the postindustrial society, often detracting from rather than promoting the commonweal. Sometimes pointing to the fragmentation and parochialism of (some) craft unions in Great Britain, this policy prescription would permit the *existence* of unions but would deny them any government encouragement or support because of their broader working-class concerns.

Most observers would disagree with these critics. Students of labor relations point to the establishment of industrial jurisprudence and industrial self-government as the primary virtue of contemporary unionism. Even if unions do distort the efficient allocation of resources in some instances, the majority tends to view the promotion of labor peace through collective bargaining as an overriding social goal. Although public policy could erect a system of employee rights and could attempt to intervene and assure workers a "fair" wage, such intervention would deny the parties directly involved a significant voice in decisions affecting daily workplace behavior. Decentralized collective bargaining provides an opportunity for the union and employer, who are directly affected and most knowledgeable about workplace conditions, to resolve their inevitable differences and cooperate. A central authority could be a substitute for unions and collective bargaining, but only at the cost of limiting local participation in workplace decisions.

If unions are defended on the basis of the worker participation they permit, the question of the "proper" union focus still remains. Should unions confine their representation role to members and their interests, or should unions act as spokesmen for the broader "working class"? The choice of a goal largely determines the instruments used to achieve that goal; if unions, for example, seek to represent the broad working class, they are forced to use political means, since unions are not represented in each plant and workplace. Unions which confine their concern to narrow member interests can rely largely on collective bargaining, since their concerns are localized.

American "business unionism" has opted for placing member interests first, relying on collective bargaining rather than political means to promote union aims. Several forces are working to change this traditional focus of American unionism. An unstable economy and increasing international interdependence have forced unions to cooperate and press for both full employment policies and policies which protect domestic jobs. A growing government work force and public sector unionism has lent an aura of respectability to union political activity. Finally, narrow business unionism can encourage union members to view the union in business terms; rather than having a union solidarity which emanates from a common worker bond, individuals can simply compare the monetary and nonmonetary costs of membership to the economic and noneconomic benefits, taking little interest in the union as an institution. To remain viable, American unions may be forced to adopt a more activist political role. While the union must still place member interests first, concerns for economic policy decisions and international interdependency may make the union of the future pursue its broadened social and economic goals through the political process, reserving its collective bargaining function to advance narrow economic interests.

Labor unions emerged as worker-generated protective devices, with "homegrown" instruments—collective bargaining, strikes, and pickets—to achieve their purposes. Initially opposed by both employers and government, unions established a foothold and demonstrated that collective bargaining was a means for peacefully resolving labor conflict. Only after unionism was established did it receive government support and encouragement, winning acceptance less than a generation ago. The intervening years have witnessed profound changes in labor relations but, even if unions and collective bargaining a generation hence only faintly resemble their contemporary counterparts, they remain a remarkable tribute to the insights of working men and women in creating and establishing a system to govern the fundamental employment relationship in society.

Bibliography

Barbash, Jack. *Trade Unions and National Economic Policy.* Baltimore, Md.: John Hopkins University Press, 1972.

A country-by-country examination of union participation in the formulation and administration of policies to combat inflation and unemployment.

Bok, D., and J. Dunlop. *Labor and the American Community.* New York: Simon & Schuster, 1970.

A survey of the American labor movement by two eminent labor specialists. The first two chapters contain the results of public opinion polls and profile union members and leaders.

Lewis, H.G. *Unionism and Relative Wages in the United States, An Empirical Inquiry.* Chicago: University of Chicago Press, 1963.

The classic survey of the union impact on relative wages. It is not clear that the impacts observed until 1963 are indicative of pressures in the 1970s.

Somers, G. "Collective Bargaining and the Social-Economic Contract." *Proceedings of the Industrial Relations Research Association,* December, 1975, pp. 1–7.

A recent president of the Industrial Relations Research Association (IRRA) argues that collective bargaining must be willing to expand in scope to accommodate the demands of today's work force and economy.

Glossary of Labor Law Terms

10

Agency shop   A clause in a union-management agreement which makes union membership optional but requires employees who decide not to join the selected union to pay union initiation fees and dues.

Arbitration   The hearing and resolution of a dispute between parties by a third person chosen by both parties. The arbitrator generally has decision-making power, but that power is limited by the agreement in force.

Bargaining unit   The group of employees represented collectively by a union in the negotiation of a collective bargaining agreement.

Boycott   Concerted action by a union against an employer, as when union members refuse to deal with that employer and when union members urge third parties to cease dealing with the struck employer, in order to induce employer bargaining concessions.

Cease-and-desist order   An order issued by a labor relations board demanding that an employer or a union abstain from an unfair labor practice.

Checkoff   The employer's deduction of initiation fees and dues (and sometimes fines and assessments) from the employee's paycheck, and the payment of the deduction to the union.

Closed shop   A plant in which all employees belong to the union and in which only union workers are hired.

Collective bargaining   The entire process of negotiation by which a union and an employer come to an agreement concerning wages, working conditions, and other bargainable issues, culminating in a contract.

Common law   The body of rules and principles, written and unwritten, which derive from tradition and universal custom. The common law was adopted from English judicial decisions at the time of the American Revolution and is applied and modified by the courts of the United States. Compare **statutory law.**

Craft union   A labor organization whose membership is restricted to persons engaged in a specific type of work or occupation.

Employee association   An organization, usually of public employees, which provides services to members and lobbies on their behalf. Many of these associations are being converted to union status.

Exclusive bargaining rights   A situation in which only the elected union can represent a group of employees for a specified time period. Workers cannot bargain individually.

Fact finding   Investigation of a dispute by an impartial individual or panel which issues a report stating the cause of the dispute. The fact finder may also issue recommendations for settling the dispute.

Featherbedding   Receiving payment for work that is not required by the employer or performing paid tasks that are not really necessary for completion of the work.

Good-faith bargaining   Negotiation with an open mind and a willingness to make reasonable efforts to reconcile differences and reach an agreement.

Grievance procedure   The structure that exists in an agreement to settle disputes that arise out of contract interpretation and application.

Hiring hall   The hiring of union workers by the employer through a central union office. The hiring hall is most prevalent where employment is intermittent. The central office tends to spread the available work around more evenly.

Industrial union   A labor organization whose membership includes all persons working in a plant or industry, regardless of the type of work they perform.

Injunction   A mandatory order issued by a court of equity to cause some action to take place or to prevent the action from taking place. It is generally a short-run measure until the problem can be adjudicated.

Labor relations   The study and practice of resolving employee-employer problems arising out of work.

Local   A group of organized workers who hold a charter from an international or national union.

Lockout   An act by an employer in which employees are prevented from working at their jobs in an effort to compel the employees to accede to the terms of employment desired by management.

Mediation   An attempt by a third party to bring disputants together by persuasion and compromise.

Multiemployer bargaining unit   The collective representation by a single union of the employees of two or more employers.

Negotiation   The discussion, deliberation, and resolution of a labor dispute directly between the involved parties.

Open shop   A plant in which an employee is not required to join the union or to pay dues to the union to maintain employment.

Picketing The patrolling of a struck establishment by union members and sympathizers carrying signs to indicate that the employer is engaged in unfair labor practices or simply to announce that a strike is in progress.

Professional association An organization composed largely of professional or white-collar employees.

Runaway shop The transfer of work to another plant or the relocation of an existing plant in order to avoid or discourage unionization.

Scab Term, meaning "traitor," applied to a nonstriking employee by fellow employees on strike; also applied to persons (called strikebreakers) hired by the employer to replace striking workers.

Secondary boycott Exertion of economic pressure by a union which threatens, coerces, or restrains a third party that continues to deal with the struck employer. This type of boycott is generally held to be illegal.

Seniority Preferential treatment based on length of service (and occasionally ability and physical fitness) given to employees in job assignments, promotions, transfers, and layoffs.

Shop steward The union representative, elected at the local level, who is in charge of handling labor's grievances with the representatives of management.

Sitdown strike An unlawful strike during which the strikers remain on the employer's property, taking possession of the property and excluding others from entry.

State right-to-work laws State statutes or constitutional provisions that prohibit the requirement of union membership as a condition of employment.

Statutory law Legislatively enacted law. Compare **common law.**

Strike A concerted stopping of work to compel an employer to agree to workers' demands or in protest against terms or conditions imposed by employment.

Sweetheart contract A contract negotiated by union leaders that provides benefits to union leaders, usually at the expense of membership benefits.

Unfair labor practice Employer and union practices inimical to the rights of employees that are forbidden by law. Remedies are available through the administrative processes of the National Labor Relations Board.

Unfair labor practice strike A strike launched in response to an unfair labor practice committed by an employer.

Union security Collective bargaining issues, such as checkoff and closed shop, in which the employer helps the union organize and maintain the work force.

Union shop A clause in a union-management agreement which provides hiring freedom to the employer but which requires that all new employees join the union within a specified period (usually thirty days) and that all employees maintain their union membership during the life of the agreement.

Wildcat strike An unauthorized strike in violation of a collective bargaining agreement for which the parent union disclaims responsibility.

Yellow-dog contract Employment contracts which require an employee to renounce all union connections and to promise not to join a union while employed under the contract.

Index

Lloyd-LaFollette Act, 106
Locals, 4, 44, 51
  coalition bargaining by, 57
  federations of, 10, 55–56
  fees and dues collected by, 57
  leadership in, 55
  structure of, 53–56
Lockouts, 4, 64, 76, 77, 79–80, 81, 87
  in labor law, 91, 93
  notice of, 69
  reserved for disputes about interests in
    contract negotiation, 64
  restricted to mandatory bargaining issues,
    90
Longshoring, 3, 78, 93
Low-wage workers, 19–20, 21, 29–30

Machinists' union, 59n
Male workers in labor force, 24, 25
Management, 2
  acceptance of unions by, 15–16, 42
  as actor in industrial relations system, 48
  arbitrary actions of, and rise of unions, 38,
    40
  bargaining power of, 77, 78
  internal bargaining by, 79
  opposed to worker voice in plant operation,
    11–12
  rights of, in collective bargaining, 67, 68
  rights of, in common law, 14–15
  and scientific management, 12
  structure of, 61
  unions opposed by, 7, 9, 12, 14, 41, 64
  use of government by, 42–43
Managers in unions, 28, 114
Manufacturing sector, 24, 26
  unions in, 18–19, 120–21
Marx, Karl, 82
Marxism, on labor movement, 45–46
Maslow, Abraham, 128
McBride, Lloyd, 60
Meany, George, 56, 59n
Mechanics Union of Trade Associations, 8
Mediation, 115
Merchant-capitalists, 8, 20, 46
Merchant-journeymen, 7–8
Middlemen, 8, 20
Miller, Arnold, 60
Mining industry, 3, 12, 81
  unions in, 18–19, 26–27
Minorities
  discrimination against, and collective
    bargaining, 122–23
  in labor force, 24

Mixed unions, 106
Mobility of labor, 39–40

National Association of Government
    Employees, 106
National Association of Letter Carriers, 110
National Association of Manufacturers,
    11–12
National Education Association, 26, 37, 107,
    109n, 111, 120
National emergency disputes, 93
National Industrial Recovery Act, 16
National Labor-Management Conference, 16
National Labor Relations Act. See Wagner
    Act
National Labor Relations Board, 14,
    16–17, 110
  on bargaining units, 66
  and jurisdictional disputes, 53
  in national emergency disputes, 93
  reform in procedures of, 121
  structure and functions of, in collective
    bargaining, 87–91
  and unfair labor practices, 94
National unions, 10, 40, 51
  and collective bargaining, 57
  decreasing number of, 57
  finances of, 57
  and industry structure concentration,
    55–56, 57
  structure of, 53–55, 56
National Wage Policy Committee, 110
National War Labor Board, 12, 17, 96
Negotiation, 1
  agreement stage in, 74
  attitudinal structuring in, 78, 79
  and bargaining power, 76–81
  consolidation stage in, 74
  and distributive bargaining, 78, 79
  grievance bargaining in, 81n
  integrative bargaining in, 78, 79
  internal bargaining in, 78, 79
  and membership ratification vote, 74
  of pattern agreements, 72, 73
  preparation for, 73
  process of, 71–76
  sets of demands in, 73
  shopping lists in, 73
  testing stage in, 73–74
  See also Collective bargaining
Nonfarm laborers, 25–26
Nonwage benefits as issue in collective
    bargaining, 18

good answers
to tough questions

About Dependence
and Separation

Written by Joy Berry

☪ CHILDRENS PRESS ®

CHICAGO

Managing Editor: Cathy Vertuca
Copy Editor: Annette Gooch
Contributing Editor: James Gough, M.D.

Art Direction: Communication Graphics
Designer: Jennifer Wiezel
Illustration Designer: Bartholomew
Inking Artist: Claudia Brown
Lettering Artist: Linda Hanney
Coloring Artist: Michele Collier
Typography and Production: Communication Graphics

Published by Childrens Press
in cooperation with Living Skills Press

This book can answer the following questions:
- How do you become dependent on other people, things, and places?
- Does your dependency change as you become older?
- How does it feel to be separated from the people, things, and places you depend on?
- What facts about separation do you need to know?
- How can you handle separation appropriately?

When you were a baby, you were helpless.

You were not able to protect yourself or provide the things you needed to survive and grow.

You depended on other **people** to keep you safe by protecting you and keeping you from harm.

When you were a baby, you depended on other **people** to meet your physical needs by making sure you had the food, water, clothing, and shelter you needed.

You also depended on them to meet your emotional needs for things such as love and respect.

When you were a baby, you most likely felt safe and secure around the people who took care of you.

When these people were not around—when you were separated from them—you might have felt frightened and insecure.

Besides depending on people, you depended on **things** that made you feel safe and secure.

For example, you might have depended on a special blanket because it kept you warm, and when you nestled under it, you felt that nothing could get to you and hurt you. The blanket might have had an odor that reminded you of the people who loved and took care of you.

You might have felt the same way about a favorite toy or some favorite clothes.

You might also have depended on **things** that helped to meet your needs.

For example, you might have depended on a baby bottle because it held the food and water that you needed. Or you might have depended on a pacifier because, like all babies, you had a need to suck, and the pacifier helped satisfy this need.

When the things you depended on were not around—when you were separated from them—you might have felt frightened.

Being separated from the things you depended on might also have caused you to feel insecure.

In addition to depending on people and things, you depended on **places** that made you feel safe and secure.

You felt protected in those places because you were used to them and you knew what to expect. You knew that nothing harmful would happen to you while you were there.

For example, when you were in your crib or playpen, you probably felt protected. You might have felt the same way about your bedroom and your family's home.

When you were not in the places you depended on—when you were separated from them—you might have felt frightened.

Being separated from the places you depended on might also have made you feel insecure.

Some people think that as a person gets older, he or she becomes totally independent.

Being totally independent means never depending on people, things, or places to protect you or meet your needs.

No one ever becomes totally independent. Everyone, no matter how old he or she is, depends on people, things, and places in one way or another.

Being dependent is a part of being human.

Of course, you will not always depend on the same things in the same way. Your dependence on people, things, and places will change as you grow and change.

For example, when you were a baby, you might have depended on a blanket to make you feel safe. But as you became older and realized your blanket could not protect you, you probably stopped depending on it for protection. Instead, you depended on it to keep you warm.

Another example of how your dependence changes as you grow and change is that when you were a baby, you depended on your parents to feed and dress you. However, as you became older and learned to feed and dress yourself, you probably stopped depending on your parents to do these things for you. Instead, you depended on them to help you do other things, such as make decisions and solve problems.

Some people think that as a person gets older, he or she becomes immune to separation.

Being immune to separation means not being affected by it. It means not being concerned or upset about being separated from a person, thing, or place you are dependent on.

No one ever becomes totally immune to separation. Everyone is dependent on something and is affected when separated from it.

Like other human beings, when you are separated from people you are dependent upon, you might feel
- **afraid** that you might get hurt because they are not around to protect you,
- **angry** that you are separated from them, and
- **insecure** because you do not know what is going to happen to you while they are gone.

You might also feel
- **worried** that something might prevent you from reuniting with them,
- **left** out because you are unable to participate in whatever they are doing, and
- **lonely** because you miss being around them.

These feelings can cause you to lose your appetite or become physically ill.

Like other human beings, when you lose something that you are dependent upon, you might feel
- **frustrated** because you cannot find the object,
- **angry** at yourself or at someone else for losing it, and
- **disappointed** that you will not be able to use the object again.

You might also feel
- **sad** that it is gone, and
- **worried** that you will not be able to replace the lost object.

When you leave a place you are dependent upon, you might feel
- **insecure** because you do not know what is going to happen to you in the new location, and
- **worried** that you won't like being in the new location.

You might also feel
- **sad** that you will be leaving the surroundings that are familiar to you, and
- **overwhelmed** and frustrated because you have to adjust to an entirely new situation.

Separation can cause you to feel uncomfortable. However, knowing some important facts about separation can help you feel better.

Fact #1: Separation is a part of life and cannot be completely avoided.

It is impossible to be around any person, thing, or place all of the time.

For example, you cannot go to work with your parents and they cannot go to school with you. Therefore, you must be separated from them some of the time.

Also, you need to go to school and other important places. Therefore, you must be separated from your home some of the time.

Fact #2: Separation can help you grow and become a better person.

Separation forces you to be without something you are dependent upon. During the separation, you learn that you can survive without the thing you have depended upon. Often, the separation helps you develop better ways to get your needs met.

For example, when you were forced to be separated from your parents, you learned that you could survive without them. You learned to develop relationships with other people, such as your friends and teachers. These new relationships most likely provided better ways to fulfill your social and educational needs.

Fact #3: Separation can help you avoid overdependence.

Overdependence is depending too much on a person, thing, or place.

You are overdependent if your dependence keeps you from doing things that you can and should do for yourself.

For example, you might become so dependent on your parents to make your decisions that you never learn to make decisions for yourself.

Or you might become so dependent on TV for entertainment that you might never develop your creativity or the ability to entertain yourself.

You are overdependent if your dependence on something controls you.

For example, you might become overdependent on a favorite article of clothing and not be able to function normally unless you are wearing it.

Or you might become overdependent on a certain bed and not be able to sleep unless you are in it.

Separating yourself from things can help you overcome your overdependence on them.

Fact #4: Resisting separation can make experiencing it more difficult.

Resisting separation is refusing to accept it or doing everything you can do to stop it from happening.

Resistance takes a lot of time and effort. Sometimes it causes a lot of pain and unhappiness.

For example, some children resist separation from their parents by throwing a tantrum. Often, the tantrum causes the parents to become angry or upset. When this happens, the child is forced to deal with the parents' uncomfortable feelings, as well as the separation.

Resisting separation in this way can cause you to spend unnecessary time, energy, and effort in throwing a tantrum and in dealing with the negative situation the tantrum causes.

Separation from the people, things, and places that you are dependent upon can cause you to feel frightened and insecure. However, separation can also cause you to grow and become a better person if you follow three important steps to handling it appropriately.

Step One: Face the separation.

Acknowledge this fact: the separation is going to happen.

Step Two: Accept the separation.

Accept this fact: There is most likely nothing you can do to stop the separation from happening.

Step Three: Do whatever is necessary to make the separation as easy as possible on everyone.

If you are ever separated from someone you are dependent upon, you can make yourself feel better by doing these things:

Find out
- how long the separation will last (when it will begin and end),
- where you will be and what you will be doing during the separation,
- where the other person will be and what he or she will be doing during the separation,
- how you will be able to contact the person, and
- when and how the person will contact you.

You can get this information by talking to your parents or to the adults who are responsible for you during the separation.

Do whatever you can do to make the separation a positive experience.

- Give the person a pleasant good-bye.
- Keep yourself busy with positive activities during the separation.
- Talk to other people about the person whenever you miss him or her.
- If possible, telephone or write letters to the person.
- Use a calendar to help you keep track of the separation (mark off each day).
- Think about the happy day when you will be getting back together with the person.

If you are temporarily separated from something you are dependent upon, you can make yourself feel better by trying not to focus on the object you are missing.

Instead, find something else to be the focus of your attention. Look for positive features of the objects you have, and try to appreciate and enjoy them.

If you should lose something you are dependent upon, you can make yourself feel better by doing your best to find it.

- Return to where you last saw the object and search for it.
- Make a thorough search of the places where you used the object.
- Ask other people to help you find the object.

If you are unable to find the object, you can make yourself feel better by doing whatever you can to get over the loss.

- Give yourself a specific amount of time to find the object and stop looking for it when the allotted time has passed.
- Figure out whether and how the object can be replaced, and then replace it as soon as possible.
- Try not to focus on the missing object. Instead, think of the things you still have and be thankful for them.

If you are temporarily separated from a place you are dependent upon, you can make yourself feel better by trying not to focus on the place you are missing.

Instead, focus your attention on the place where you are. Look for positive features of the place and try to appreciate and enjoy them.

If you should have to move from a home you have become dependent upon, you can make yourself feel better by learning all you can about your new home and neighborhood *before* you move.

Find out about the
- school you will attend,
- church or synagogue you might attend, and
- community programs and activities available to people your age.

You can learn about your new community by visiting it or by contacting its chamber of commerce for information.

Do whatever you can to make the move go as smoothly as possible.

Do these things before you move:

- Get the addresses and telephone numbers of your special friends and neighbors so you can keep in touch with them.
- Collect photographs and mementos from the community you will be leaving. Store these items in a scrapbook or special box.
- Help your family pack. Be sure to pack your own belongings.

Do these things after you move:

- Unpack your own belongings and set up your own bedroom.
- Make new friends and get involved in your community as soon as possible.
- Concentrate on what you like about the new community.
- Telephone or write letters to your special friends and neighbors from the old community.
- Look at photographs and mementos from the old community.

When dealing with dependence and separation, it is important for you to remember that you have within you the ability to get everything you need to survive and grow.

Being separated from the things you depend on can cause you to become more independent.

As you become more independent, you will most likely become a happier, healthier, more productive person.